Urban Land Institute

AF702767

SCORCHED

Extreme Heat and Real Estate

AUTHORS

Katharine Burgess
Vice President, Urban Resilience
Urban Land Institute

Elizabeth Foster
Senior Associate, Urban Resilience
Urban Land Institute

ULI MEMBER REVIEWERS

Janice Barnes, PhD
Principal and Director of Resilience
Waggonner & Ball

Ladd Keith, PhD
Planning Lecturer and Chair of the Sustainable Built Environment Program
University of Arizona

ULI PROGRAM STAFF

Billy Grayson
Executive Director, Center for Sustainability and Economic Performance

Rachel MacCleery
Senior Vice President
Content

Bridget Stesney
Senior Director
Building Healthy Places

Matt Norris
Senior Manager
Building Healthy Places

Leah Sheppard
Senior Associate
Urban Resilience

Kate Donatelli
Intern
Urban Resilience

Megan (French) Palathra
Intern
Urban Resilience

ULI PROJECT STAFF

James A. Mulligan
Senior Editor

Laura Glassman, Publications Professionals LLC
Manuscript Editor

Brandon Weil
Art Director

Thomas Cameron
Designer

Craig Chapman
Senior Director
Publishing Operations

COVER PHOTO: Los Angeles downtown cityscape at sunset. (Shutterstock)

2001 L Street, NW | Suite 200 | Washington, DC 20036-4948

Recommended bibliographic listing: Burgess, Katharine, and Elizabeth Foster. *Scorched: Extreme Heat and Real Estate.* Washington, DC: Urban Land Institute, 2019.

ISBN: 978-0-87420-431-5

ABOUT THE URBAN LAND INSTITUTE

The Urban Land Institute is a global, member-driven organization comprising more than 44,000 real estate and urban development professionals dedicated to advancing the Institute's mission of providing leadership in the responsible use of land and in creating and sustaining thriving communities worldwide.

ULI's interdisciplinary membership represents all aspects of the industry, including developers, property owners, investors, architects, urban planners, public officials, real estate brokers, appraisers, attorneys, engineers, financiers, and academics. Established in 1936, the Institute has a presence in the Americas, Europe, and the Asia Pacific region, with members in 80 countries.

More information is available at uli.org. Follow ULI on Twitter, Facebook, LinkedIn, and Instagram.

CONTRIBUTORS

ULI is grateful to The JPB Foundation for its support of this project and ULI's Urban Resilience Program. ULI also appreciates and is honored by the volunteer contributions to this report of more than 50 subject matter experts from ULI's membership and beyond.

RESEARCH PROCESS

To better understand how heat could impact real estate and land use, ULI's Urban Resilience program interviewed more than 50 real estate developers, designers, land use policymakers, and climate scientists.

A full list of the organizations of those who shared their knowledge and perspectives in interviews, nominated case studies, and provided supporting materials for this report is provided in the Acknowledgments.

SHUTTERSTOCK

CONTENTS

An iconic 125-foot-tall shade sail at SkySong, the Arizona State University Innovation Center, anchors the 42-acre development and is part of a heat-conscious design that helps attract tenants and reflects the founding partners' forward-thinking, entrepreneurial vision.

EXECUTIVE SUMMARY

Heat is the number-one natural disaster killer in this country.

DANIEL HOMSEY
Director of Neighborhood Resilience, City and County of San Francisco

Soaring temperatures and dangerous heat waves are the uncomfortable reality in communities across the United States. Extreme heat risks are not limited to historically hot environments or summer months; heat is the most widespread and deadly weather-related hazard in the United States.[1] With the projected impacts of climate change and continued urban development, many communities are likely to experience higher-temperature days; longer, more frequent heat waves; and intensified impacts in cities where "urban heat islands" (UHIs) form because of the heat-absorbing properties of urban surfaces.

Urban areas are the most at-risk locations from extreme heat in the United States. This heat has the potential for devastating public health consequences—as seen in the Chicago Heat Wave of 1995, the European heat wave of 2003, and more recently, the near global summer heat wave of 2018. Extreme heat also has the potential for long-term impacts on local economies and consumer market preferences.

In response, U.S. real estate developers, designers, and policymakers increasingly acknowledge the consequences of extreme heat and are seeking solutions to make buildings, neighborhoods, parks, and outdoor spaces more adaptable to environmental conditions and comfortable for occupants. Although managing extreme heat has no one-size-fits-all approach, particularly given different humidity levels and other local conditions, a suite of potential options is available, many of which also build amenity value and address other environmental needs such as stormwater management. Broadly, developments can prevent the absorption of heat with light-colored surfaces and materials, provide direct cooling with increased shade from built and natural shade canopies, and better cope with extremes through "heat-aware" building envelopes and heating, ventilation, and air conditioning (HVAC) choices that stabilize indoor temperatures even during power outages.

Policymakers are considering how to address extreme heat in land use and building regulations as well as through social services and emergency preparedness. Urban greening programs and community resources to protect the most affected demographics are well-established approaches. New programs and technologies are seeking to better understand and apply the nuances of urban heat dynamics to planning policies that can improve climate resilience through extreme heat mitigation and adaptation.

The built environment is ultimately both a contributor to and a solution for extreme heat, especially in cities, and presents numerous opportunities for mitigation and adaptation at the building and neighborhood scales. Although designing for extreme heat is an emerging issue that is not yet mainstream in many U.S. markets, it is likely to become more prevalent as extreme heat increases and is acknowledged by both consumers and local regulators and as economic, infrastructural, and public health impacts make the risks of extreme heat more visible.

This report explores how extreme heat is emerging as a growing risk factor and planning consideration across the United States and why this trend is likely to continue. The report also explores how the land use, design, and real estate sectors are responding with design approaches, technologies, and new policies to mitigate the infrastructure impacts of extreme heat and to protect human health.

Heat, especially in our market during the hot and humid months, is top of mind.

BRYAN MOLL
Executive Vice President of Development, JBG Smith

PROJECTED SUMMER TEMPERATURE
BY 2080–2099

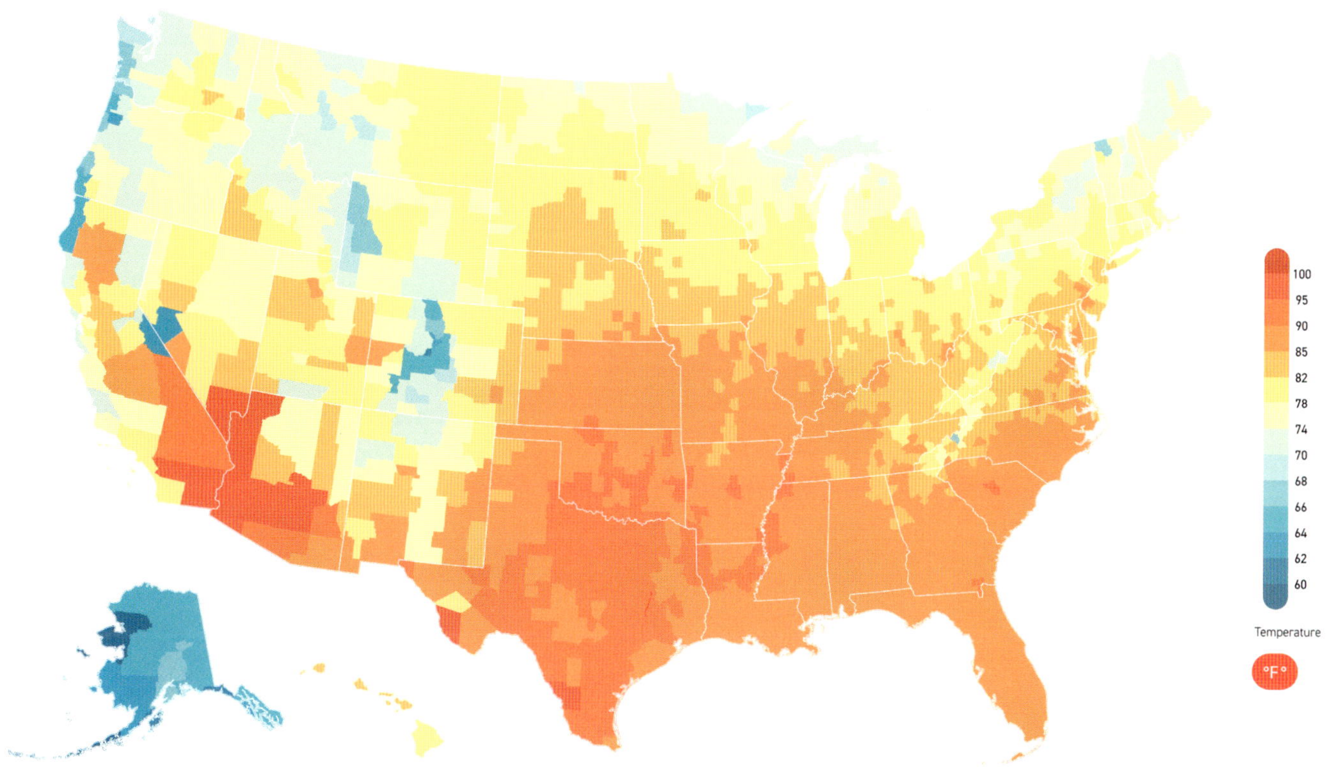

This map displays the average U.S. summer temperatures projected by the end of the century (2080–2099) if climate change continues at a rapid rate (emissions scenario RCP 8.5). (Climate Impact Lab 2019)

The exterior of the ENR2 building in Tucson is covered in a "blind" that filters direct sunlight and prevents solar heat gain. This exterior has helped reduce the building's summertime energy use by 40 percent. Find more details at developingresilience.uli.org.

> This is a conversation about the success of cities addressing heat. Each and every property has a role in that success.
>
> RIVES TAYLOR
> Principal and Codirector of Resilience, Gensler

KEY TAKEAWAYS

More cities in the United States are or will be at risk of extreme heat because of climate change and increased urban development. High temperatures are already influential factors in real estate design, construction, and maintenance in the Southeast, Southwest, California, and increasingly, in the Northeast; moreover, the scientific consensus is that temperatures are continuing to increase in these locations. Rising temperatures, heat waves, and urban heat islands are not limited to warm environments. The relative change in temperature causes more damage—to people, infrastructure, and landscapes—in cooler places and where fewer heat-mitigation and adaptation strategies are in place.

Extreme heat is a pressing public health risk, particularly for low-income and elderly communities. Extreme heat compromises human cardiovascular and respiratory systems and causes the greatest damage in populations with other vulnerabilities, such as preexisting health conditions or lack of available coping strategies. Cool design strategies, combined with public health and effective emergency responses, can offset heat-related mortality to a significant degree.

Without intervention, the current and potential future impacts of extremely high temperatures—on real estate developments, infrastructure, and the economy—could be substantial. Implications relate to the durability of building materials, energy demand and consumption, outdoor space design, consumer location preferences and amenity expectations, regulation and taxation, and practitioners' insurance costs and professional liability risks. Many of these implications could ultimately impact real estate development projects' net present value.

Leading developers and designers are focused on creating ways to make buildings simultaneously more adaptable to external high temperatures and more comfortable for occupants. Thermal comfort design approaches include increasing shade through built or natural canopies; choosing reflective materials; integrating vegetation cover onto buildings; implementing energy efficiency strategies; and using passive cooling, wind channeling, and sometimes air conditioning. Some industry leaders are designing for heat projections for the 50-year lifetime of a building, taking into account projected temperature increases caused by climate change and urbanization.

Heat-related land use policies often support other city goals related to greenhouse gas (GHG) emissions reduction, stormwater management, public health improvement, decreased social inequity, and effective emergency response. Heat-related policies involve building safety and efficiency standards, urban greening, public space design, and provision of social services. These policies have the potential to significantly reduce urban heat island effects, thereby decreasing temperatures, improving quality of life, and preventing infrastructure damage in metropolitan areas. Investments in addressing extreme heat also support public health by protecting communities who are most vulnerable, including the elderly, the young, and low-income households.

Some interventions addressing extreme heat can be counterproductive to long-term "heat resilience." In many markets, a key extreme heat response may be more widespread air conditioning, which can be costly for developers and consumers. Air conditioners give off heat and may increase local temperatures and, through the emission of greenhouse gases, perpetuate climate change.

DEFINING EXTREMES

This report uses "extreme heat" as a relative term to refer to conditions above a location's baseline normal temperatures as well as to the extreme temperature during heat waves.

The real estate sector can improve "extreme heat resilience" through *mitigation* (strategies that directly reduce temperatures) as well as *adaptation* (actions that help people and businesses cope with the impacts of extreme heat).

Over the long term, extreme heat could impact consumer preferences as well as economic opportunities in various markets. Research suggests that extreme heat is likely to impact U.S. gross domestic product (GDP). There is considerable speculation among investors, developers, and public officials about whether, how, and when extreme heat–related risks could influence market dynamics either directly (i.e., decrease in investment capital or reduced asset values) or through secondary channels such as increased wildfire and drought risk.

> To design for yesterday's temperature is not our only responsibility; we need to design for the future as well.
>
> TAMAR WARBURG
> Director of Sustainability and Resilience, Sasaki

DISASTER RESILIENCE AND EXTREME HEAT

Extreme heat is a dangerous hazard by itself, and it worsens other hazards. High temperatures increase the likelihood, duration, and intensity of wildfires, droughts, and smog. Heat is also a factor in electrical grid stability; high temperatures stress utility infrastructure when demand is highest. Further, extreme heat exacerbates public health issues (especially cardiovascular and respiratory problems), impacts the effectiveness of certain medicine, and reduces the body's ability to cool itself.

Many public health and emergency response officials worry about a confluence of events—an extreme heat event and simultaneous widespread power outage that leaves people without air conditioning and complicates emergency response efforts, for example. Implementing heat-mitigation features that reduce temperatures day-to-day also increases resilience by helping prevent infrastructure failures and safeguarding lives during extreme and co-occurring events.

Resilience is the capacity of a system (such as a building, business, community, or city) to prevent, withstand, respond to, and recover from a disruption. There are different types of resilience; social, engineering, disaster, and financial resilience are most closely related to extreme heat and real estate.

Rising temperatures are directly tied to an increase in the number, duration, and severity of wildfires.

PART I

THE SCIENCE AND IMPACTS

Like many historically temperate cities, New York City faces increasingly frequent and hotter extreme heat events. High temperatures are made worse in urban areas like New York City that experience the urban heat island effect.

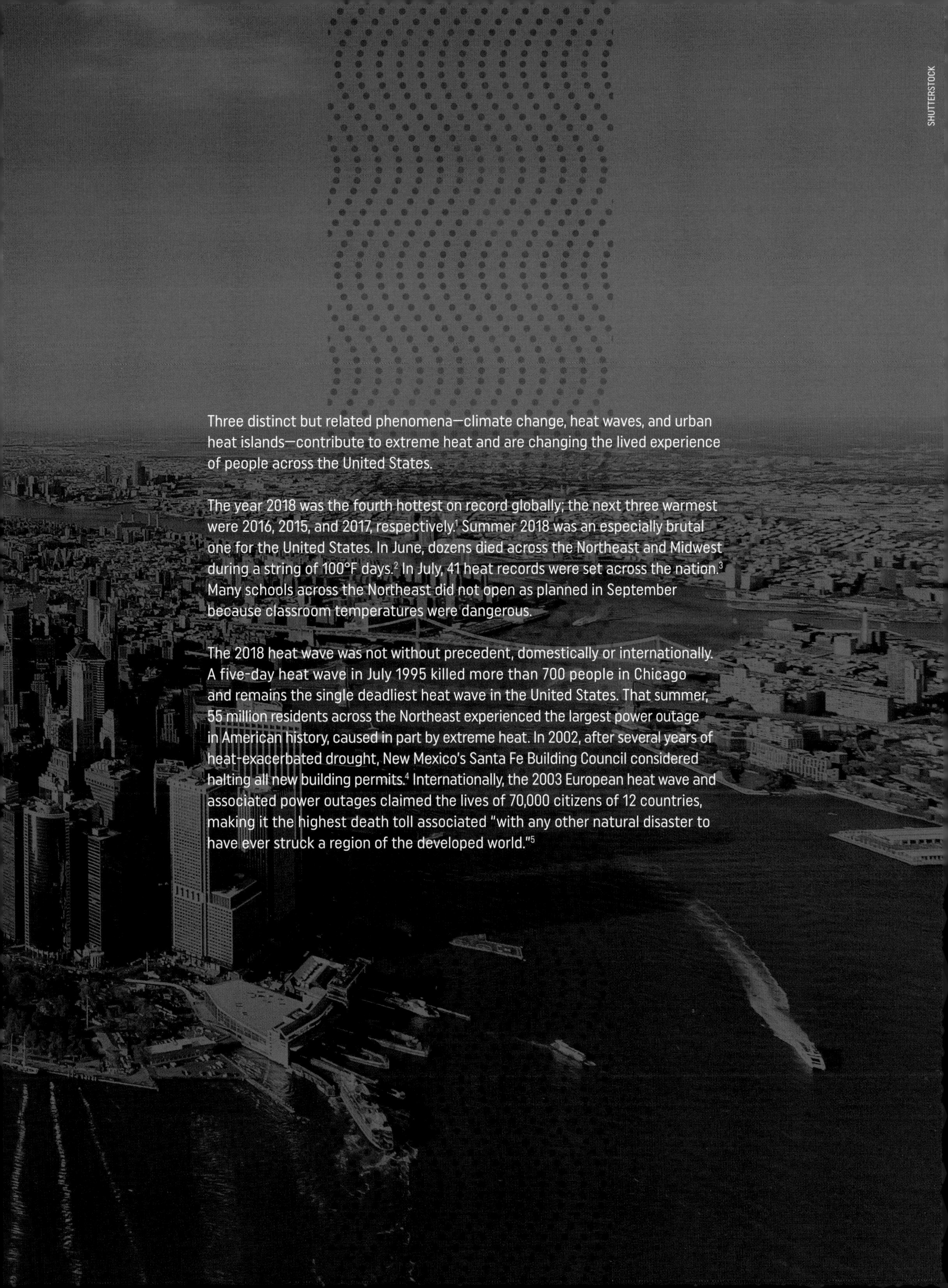

SHUTTERSTOCK

Three distinct but related phenomena—climate change, heat waves, and urban heat islands—contribute to extreme heat and are changing the lived experience of people across the United States.

The year 2018 was the fourth hottest on record globally; the next three warmest were 2016, 2015, and 2017, respectively.[1] Summer 2018 was an especially brutal one for the United States. In June, dozens died across the Northeast and Midwest during a string of 100°F days.[2] In July, 41 heat records were set across the nation.[3] Many schools across the Northeast did not open as planned in September because classroom temperatures were dangerous.

The 2018 heat wave was not without precedent, domestically or internationally. A five-day heat wave in July 1995 killed more than 700 people in Chicago and remains the single deadliest heat wave in the United States. That summer, 55 million residents across the Northeast experienced the largest power outage in American history, caused in part by extreme heat. In 2002, after several years of heat-exacerbated drought, New Mexico's Santa Fe Building Council considered halting all new building permits.[4] Internationally, the 2003 European heat wave and associated power outages claimed the lives of 70,000 citizens of 12 countries, making it the highest death toll associated "with any other natural disaster to have ever struck a region of the developed world."[5]

THE SCIENCE OF EXTREME HEAT

Climate change has caused an increase in temperature across the United States and makes extreme heat events hotter and more likely to occur.[6] In addition, climate change is not the only cause of extreme heat—and in cities, not even the main cause of these more intense, frequent, and long-lasting extreme heat events. Several distinct but related climate- and weather-related phenomena contribute to extreme heat:

- Rising global temperatures (a long-term increase caused by human-induced climate change);
- Heat waves (relatively short-term periods of abnormally hot and humid weather); and
- Urban heat islands (areas of hotter temperatures created by local, urban conditions).

The relative change in temperature causes more damage—to people and infrastructure—in cooler places and where fewer adaptation strategies (such as air conditioning or shade trees) are in place.

URBAN HEAT ISLANDS—NOT GLOBAL WARMING—CAUSE THE MAJORITY OF THE TEMPERATURE RISE IN U.S. CITIES. CITIES ARE 2° TO 6°F WARMER ON AVERAGE THAN THEIR SURROUNDINGS AND ARE WARMING UP TO 50 PERCENT FASTER THAN THE REST OF THE COUNTRY.[7]

The UHI-induced temperature increase above the "baseline normal" and the faster rate of warming are in addition to the "background" 1° to 2°F rise in global temperatures that has already occurred in the United States because of climate change.

> While we are in a northern climate, we still have significant heat issues during the summer.
>
> SHAYNA STOTT
> Environmental Planner, Toronto City Planning

BROKEN TEMPERATURE RECORDS
SUMMER 2018

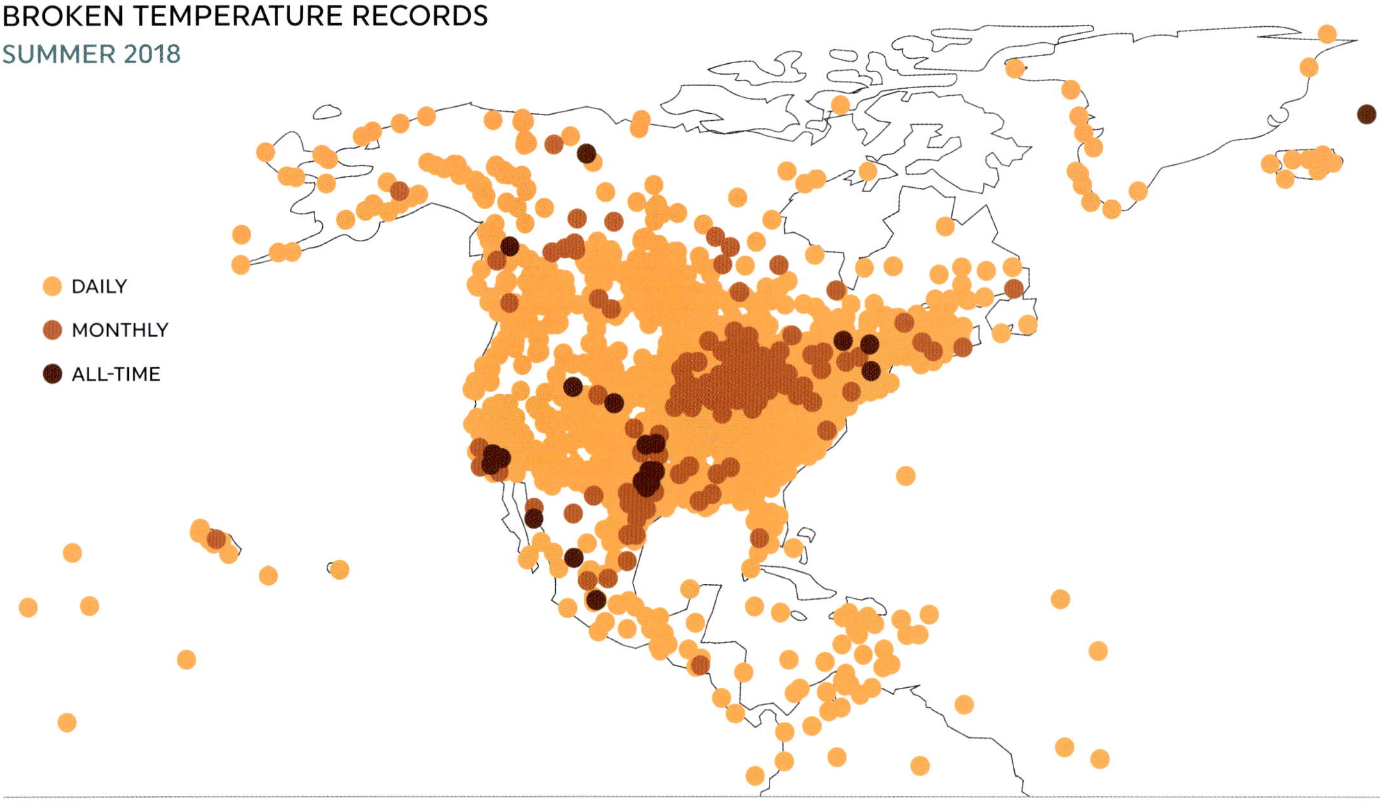

This map displays the daily, monthly, and all-time-high temperature records broken between May 1 and July 31, 2018, during an uncommonly warm summer. (ULI, adapted from Axios with data from Berkeley Earth)

HEAT WAVE SURFACE TEMPERATURES

SAN FRANCISCO, SEPTEMBER 1, 2017

HIGH
145.13 degrees Fahrenheit

TEMPERATURE DIFFERENCE
OF 78 DEGREES

LOW
66.29 degrees Fahrenheit

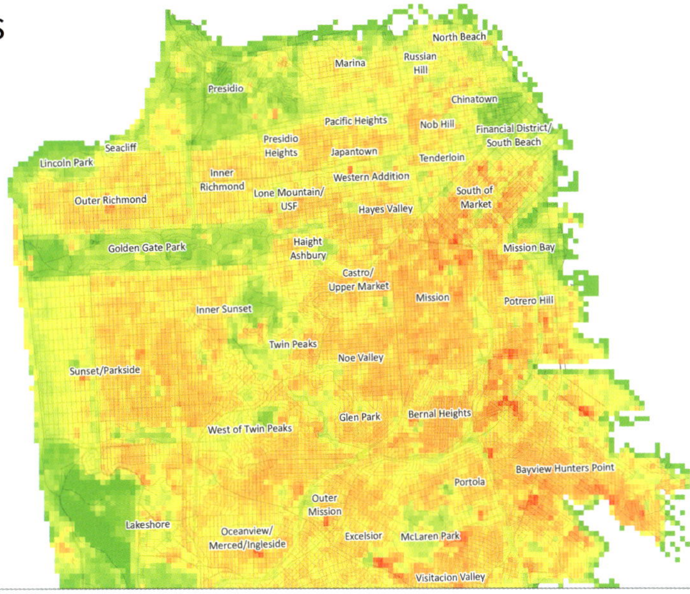

The temperature difference across San Francisco during this September 2017 heat event was 78.84°F, demonstrating the significant influence of land use and topography on temperature. (San Francisco Office of Neighborhood Resilience)

Elements of Extreme Heat

Although these three extreme heat factors (climate change, heat waves, and urban heat islands) are each distinct phenomena, many of their causes and consequences are the same.

CLIMATE CHANGE

Climate change has caused a 1.3° to 1.9°F temperature increase in the United States since record keeping began; within several decades, U.S. average temperatures are projected to be 2° to 4°F higher with even larger temperature increases expected in some regions.[8] What the U.S. climate will be by the end of the century depends in large part upon the rates of GHG emissions that drive climate change. "There's nowhere in the U.S. right now where temperature and humidity levels are so high that a healthy individual cannot stay outside for long without becoming ill or dying, but in 20 years, it's possible," says Brian Stone, renowned heat expert and program director at Georgia Tech's School of City and Regional Planning.

HEAT WAVES

In addition to the background increase in temperature, climate change is altering the characteristics of extreme heat events. "It's not just excessive heat," explains Rives Taylor, principal and codirector of resilience at Gensler; "it's the extreme swing in temperature from one day to the next. That sudden difference in temperature wreaks havoc on mechanical systems and facade materiality. . . . Our buildings have to face a totally different world."

The frequency of heat waves, their duration, and the temperatures during them are all becoming more extreme. Cities today have on average 10 more extreme heat events per year than they did in the mid-1950s.[9] Heat waves also manifest differently indoors than they do outdoors.[10] Early research results indicate that, when a heat wave occurs, indoor temperatures spike later than outdoor temperatures and last longer, likely because it takes time for heat to transfer indoors, and once there, it is trapped inside.[11]

URBAN HEAT ISLANDS

Cities are at elevated risk from extreme temperatures because they absorb more of the sun's energy (i.e., heat) and can be up to 22°F hotter in comparison to their surroundings.[12] This *difference* in *temperature* between urban areas and their rural surroundings is called an *urban heat island* or the *urban heat island effect* (UHIE). UHIs are not uniform across cities; developments without significant vegetation and larger paved areas (parking lots, for example) can lead to "micro-urban heat islands."

> **You have to design for not necessarily the best-case scenario but what the temperature reality can be and what can happen on the site over time.**
>
> SETH ATWELL
> Principal, TBG Partners

Causes of Urban Heat Islands

The higher temperatures present in urban areas are the result of four factors related to building and urban design.

LAND USE CHANGE

Land development, including the removal of trees and green space and the addition of heat-absorbing materials, is an important driver of temperature change in cities. For example, the master-planned community of Columbia, Maryland, had temperature variations of only 2°F in the early stages of the town's existence in the 1960s. About six years later, after significant development and construction, the city's temperature variation was 13°F.[13] National urban tree cover across the United States is approximately 40 percent with alarming losses in cities and more than 45 states showing a declining trend in tree cover since 2009.[14]

WASTE HEAT EMISSIONS

Waste heat (mainly from energy use in buildings and transportation) also increases temperature. Waste heat emissions are significant enough to alter temperature in downtown cores on a weekly basis; Saturdays and Sundays, particularly in the morning, can have lower temperatures because fewer people are driving in and traveling around downtown.[15] Early research suggests that waste heat generated in cities not only contributes to local heat islands but has also increased temperatures regionally in the northernmost U.S. states (as well as in northern Asia) by approximately 2°F.[16]

AIR POLLUTION

Air pollution and UHIs intensify each other. The warmer air (which has more particulate matter) and suppressed wind (which helps heat dissipate) associated with UHIs create ideal conditions for smog formation. Smog then

We need to continue to make buildings as energy efficient as possible for operational and climate change purposes, but also because the more inefficient buildings are, the more heat they emit.

PATRICK HAMILTON
Director, Global Change Initiatives, Science Museum of Minnesota

URBAN HEAT ISLAND PROFILE

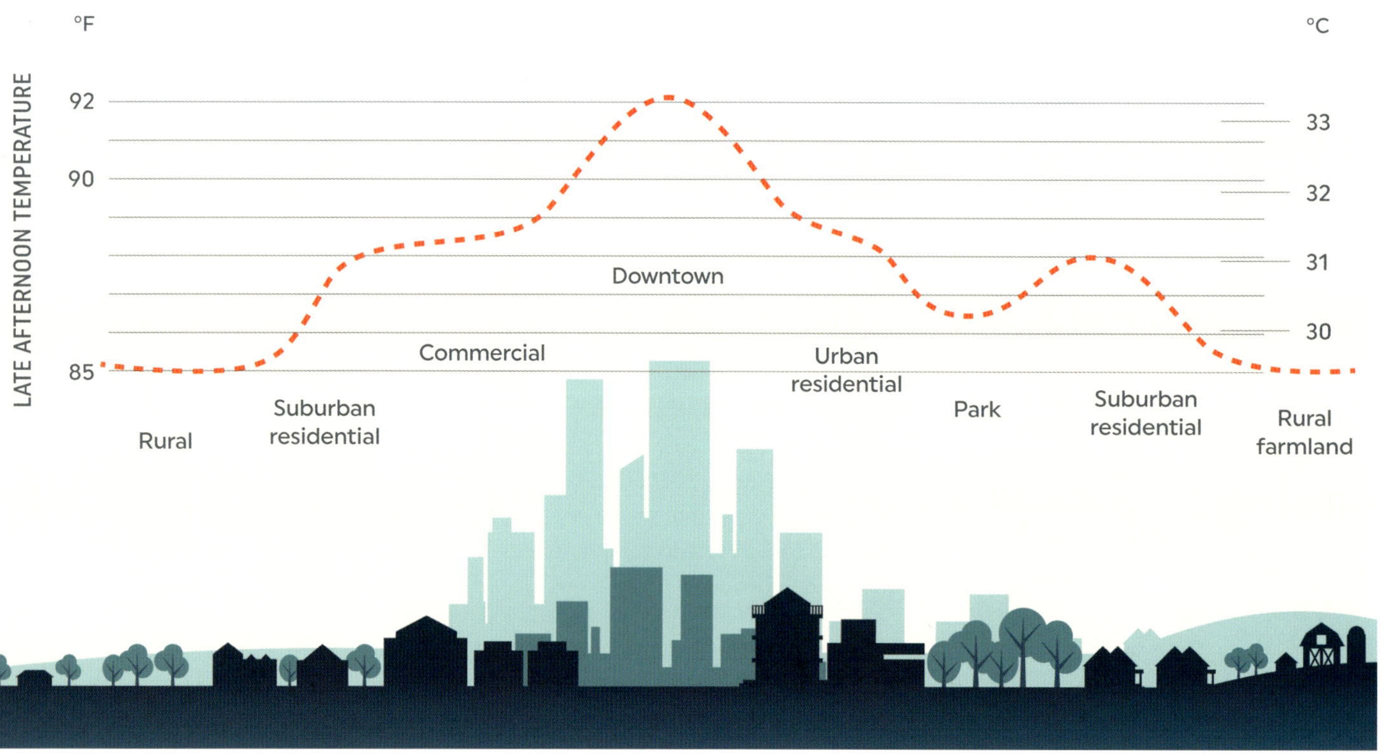

The average air temperature of a city with 1 million or more people can be 1.8° to 5.4°F warmer on average and as much as 22°F hotter at night than surrounding areas because of the urban heat island effect.[17] (Heat Island Group, Lawrence Berkeley National Laboratory, 2019)

acts as a heat-trapping barrier, exacerbating the effect. Heat islands are responsible for 20 percent of urban smog formation; implementing temperature reduction measures will also improve air quality.[18]

URBAN GEOMETRY

The characteristics of a city and its buildings influence temperature and heat distribution. The texture of a city—the pattern in which its streets and buildings are arranged—as well as the size and shape of a city are influential determinants of UHI intensity.[19] Many building types can both contribute to and mitigate the urban heat island effect. For example, tall buildings create shade (cooling effect) but also trap heat between them and slow or block wind speeds (heating effect). Urban heat islands are not all created equal; an urban area's density, layout, and building types influence local extreme heat dynamics, as do local climate, geographic features, and the surrounding natural environment.

BUILDING HEIGHT AND HEAT DISSIPATION

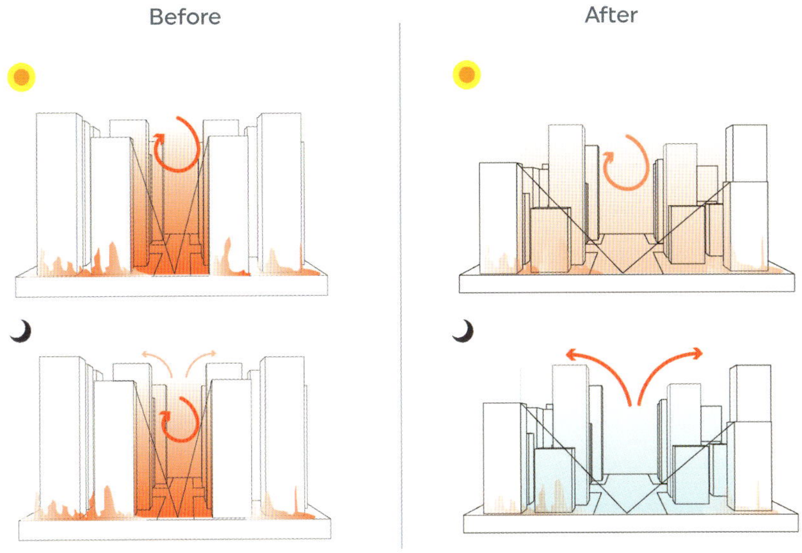

The diagram shows how taller buildings prevent streets from cooling at night and how building height could be modified to allow heat dissipation. (NYIT Urban Design Climate Lab 2017)

Even temperate and cold locations—such as Denver (above)—can experience a significant urban heat island effect. While a few extra degrees may be welcome in wintertime, higher temperatures are a summertime challenge and health hazard, especially for locations with few mitigation and adaptation strategies.

THE IMPACTS OF EXTREME HEAT

The current and projected impacts of extremely high temperatures—on people, on the economy, and on infrastructure—are substantial. In Los Angeles, public health officials have started to regularly record wintertime heat-related deaths;[20] in June 2017, American Airlines canceled over 40 flights departing Phoenix because daytime highs of 120°F were too hot for regional jets to take off;[21] and in summer 2018, roofing material across western Europe melted.[22]

> We need to concentrate investments and physical improvements in areas that have high heat risk.
>
> KIZZY CHARLES-GUZMAN
> Deputy Director, NYC Mayor's Office of Resiliency

TOP 10 MOST INTENSE URBAN HEAT ISLANDS (2004–2013)

WORST DAYTIME UHIE	WORST NIGHTTIME UHIE
1. Las Vegas	1. Las Vegas
2. Albuquerque	2. Albuquerque
3. Denver	3. Portland
4. Portland	4. Washington, D.C.
5. Louisville	5. San Diego
6. Washington, D.C.	6. Louisville
7. Kansas City	7. Phoenix
8. Columbus	8. Buffalo
9. Minneapolis	9. Minneapolis
10. Seattle	10. Philadelphia

Which U.S. cities have the worst UHIs? The rankings depend on what you measure. The ranking of cities with the worst daytime UHIE is not the same list as cities with the worst nighttime UHIE. Ranked by the average daily urban–rural temperature difference over 10 years, the 10 cities with the worst UHIs are located all over the country.

Source: ULI with data from Climate Central.

DISPARATE IMPACT OF EXTREME HEAT

Like many other environmental health issues, the impacts of extreme heat are felt disproportionally across society. Unequally vulnerable communities include those who are challenged by poverty or homelessness, elderly, young, pregnant, or socially isolated and who have preexisting medical conditions. The impacts of extreme heat are also unequally associated with African American, Latino, Asian, and First Nation communities. Outdoor workers (such as maintenance, construction, and farm workers) are routinely exposed to extreme heat with little respite, given the nature of their work.

"Hot spots" exist within the built environment where heat-related deaths and air pollution effects are more likely to occur; African Americans are 52 percent more likely than Caucasians to live in these areas of unnatural "heat risk–related land cover," Asians are 32 percent more likely, and Latinos 21 percent.[23]

Low-income communities in the United States are often underserved by green spaces that can mitigate urban heat and by civic amenities such as cooling facilities because of discriminatory land use policies and lack of investment in historically marginalized communities. For example, a heat vulnerability and heat illness assessment conducted in 2017 for Richmond, Virginia, correlated areas of high heat vulnerability with historically redlined (subject to discriminatory mortgage lending rate policies) areas.[24] Low-income communities are also less likely to have access to air conditioning and cooler recreational facilities such as swimming pools or gyms, notes Cindy Stotler, executive director of Phoenix Housing.

"As a community development corporation, we are trying to figure out how we deal with [heat] and there is no one formula," says Philip Giffee, the executive director of Neighborhood of Affordable Housing, a Boston-based community development corporation. "It is not just building stock, but also emergency preparedness and social cohesion. . . . How do you address this issue in an equitable way?"

The highly trafficked Third Avenue in the Gowanus neighborhood of Brooklyn in New York City has the characteristics of a "hot spot" where the lack of shade and concentration of dark, impervious surfaces create a microclimate of hotter temperatures and a location where pedestrians are more exposed to extreme heat.

In Los Angeles, for every 1.8°F that the temperature rises above 71.6°F, smog increases by 5 percent.[25]

IMPACTS OF EXTREME HEAT

ISSUE	IMPACTS
PUBLIC HEALTH	
 SHUTTERSTOCK	More than 65,000 people in the United States visit emergency rooms each summer for acute heat illness,[26] and about 650 die from heat-related causes each year.[27] However, widespread agreement exists that the number of heat-related deaths in the country is underestimated due to underreporting. By 2050, there could be 3,000 to 5,000 annual heat-related deaths in the United States if the current level of GHG emissions continues.[28] Higher human mortality and reduced quality of life are associated with heat waves that have higher temperatures—especially at night; have higher humidity levels; are earlier in the summer; are of longer duration; and are associated with more rapid changes in temperature. Mortality from all causes spikes in cities by 7 to 14 percent on extremely hot days.[29]
ECONOMY	
GDP	Rising temperatures could reduce overall growth of U.S. economic output one-third by 2100 because of a range of factors including impacts to labor productivity, increases in health care (and potentially health care insurance) costs, effects on agricultural outputs, and changes in consumption patterns.[30]
Municipal finance	In November 2017, Moody's Investors Service announced, "a growing negative credit factor for issuers without sufficient [climate change] adaptation and mitigation strategies."[31] In the announcement, Moody's lists risk from "climbing global temperatures" and "more frequent droughts and severe heat waves."[32] In January 2019, Fitch Ratings made a similar announcement; S&P Global says it has "long considered Environmental, Social, and Governance factors in its credit ratings" and in May 2019 released its first climate disclosure report, joining a growing number of firms voluntarily following the Task Force on Climate-Related Financial Disclosures recommendations.[33]
Labor and productivity	The largest economic losses from climate change in the United States are predicted to come from lost labor productivity—for both indoor and outdoor workers.[34] Outside, high temperatures threaten worker health (33 percent of occupational heat-related deaths occur in the construction industry) and shorten the construction season, delaying development and raising costs.[35] Indoors, extreme temperatures and poor ventilation decrease productivity and workplace satisfaction.
Retail and tourism	High temperatures can change traditional consumer shopping habits and tourist activities, decreasing sales and activity in some sectors and locations and spiking them in others. Heat-related weather events also have high costs; the 2017 California wildfires damaged millions of dollars' worth of retail structures, decreased retail and restaurant foot traffic by 40 percent, and prevented millions in potential retail sales.[36]

It's hard to imagine prominent tourist and shopping destinations without crowds, but extreme heat could drive visitors to more comfortable destinations, creating opportunities in some sectors and negative economic consequences in others.

SHUTTERSTOCK

ISSUE	IMPACTS
INFRASTRUCTURE	
Utilities	High energy demand during extreme heat events disrupts power plant operations and transmission capability, potentially leading to power outages; utility disruptions in the United States tripled between the 1990s and the 2000s.[37] Rising temperatures are expected to significantly increase cooling demand and costs to consumers nationwide. Further, if increased cooling demand is met by fossil fuel sources, the GHG emissions from those sources would continue to cause climate change and thus increase temperature.
New York City streets were dark in August 2003, during the largest blackout in U.S. history, which cost an estimated $10 billion and affected 50 million people in eight Northeast states.[38] A cascade of events and failed alarm systems led to the blackout, which was exacerbated by high temperatures and high demand for cooling.	 SHUTTERSTOCK
Transportation	Heat is already causing significant damage to road, public transit, and air infrastructure throughout the United States. Overheating of materials leads to physical damage (such as roads buckling or rail track kinking), system interruptions, and safety concerns. Other transportation impacts occur because heat decreases people's ability and willingness to use certain forms of transit.
ENVIRONMENTAL	
Peak events	Extreme heat increases the likelihood of other weather-related events, such as wildfire and drought. Since 1984, for example, the area burned by wildfires across the western United States was twice what would have burned had climate change not occurred.[39]
Species migrations	High temperatures have altered and will likely continue to alter plant and animal species' geographic ranges because of habitat changes. Species shifts challenge landscape architects and facilities teams to evaluate the hardiness of plant species and to consider whether historic native vegetation will survive over the long term.
Sasaki partnered with a Lady Bird Johnson Wildflower Center ecologist to select plant species that could survive Texas's extremely high temperatures and occasional drought-time watering bans in the Dell Medical District at the University of Texas.	 SASAKI
Water management	Rising temperatures decrease stormwater quality; pavements that are 100°F can elevate initial rainwater temperature from 70°F to over 95°F, ultimately raising the temperature of natural waterways, negatively affecting aquatic species and increasing the difficulty of managing stormwater and landscapes.[40] On a larger scale, rising temperatures from climate change contribute to sea level rise, endangering coastal communities and properties.

PART II

IMPLICATIONS AND OPPORTUNITIES FOR THE REAL ESTATE SECTOR

While the impact of extreme heat on the U.S. real estate market overall has not been quantified, the costs to specific "pieces" of the real estate industry are well documented. In this image, white and light-colored roofs on many of the buildings in Las Vegas mitigate the harmful effects of the city's significant urban heat island effect.

Extreme heat is an issue with increasing relevance to the real estate and land use sectors because of the intensifying impacts of climate change and the urban heat island effect, changes in amenity expectations and market demands in some regions, and the growing interest of regulators. In response, some developers, designers, and other land use professionals are addressing temperature-related risks through the life cycle of a building or development—from investment to construction to operations and maintenance.

Investing in heat-mitigation technology and approaches can lead to a host of benefits, such as

- improved tenant experience,
- reduced operating costs,
- improved likelihood of business continuity,
- enhanced branding, and
- additional foot traffic in pedestrian and retail environments.

SHUTTERSTOCK

Interest is growing across real estate and land use disciplines in understanding how extreme heat may influence local real estate markets and the long-term economic vitality of cities and regions. Given the effects on tenants and occupants, infrastructure, operating costs, and consumer behavior, there is risk that devaluation could occur because of extreme heat, but limited research to date has explored this question. Forward-thinking developers, investors, and designers are thinking about the potential impacts of extreme heat on their projects and portfolios and are taking action to mitigate current heat-related risks and future-proof against potential future ones.

Heat-mitigation has traditionally been considered indirectly or secondary to other real estate sustainability goals such as energy conservation and GHG emissions reduction. David Mercuris, senior vice president and development director of Goldenberg Development, summarizes that perspective, "As a general matter, we talk about the urban heat island from an energy and landscaping standpoint." Heat is then addressed through investments in HVAC efficiency and green infrastructure.

The exception to that approach is in the American Southeast and Southwest where cool design elements are the norm. "Even if it's not called out specifically," elaborates Chris Calott, developer and architect with Infill Solutions and Calott + Gifford Architecture, "when designing buildings in hot climates, designers take into consideration solar orientation, the siting of buildings, and thermal barriers and insulation. Passive solar techniques for blocking sun are very well rehearsed and pro forma from the standpoint of design practitioners in hot climates."

However, even these hot-weather experts are beginning to adjust their practices to deal with new baseline normal and extreme conditions.

NOTABLE NUMBERS

$1 BILLION — The amount saved through avoided electricity use if all commercial buildings in the U.S. switched from dark to light roofs[1]

$0.50 PER SF — The amount by which cool roofs provide average yearly net savings (including the price premium for cool roofing products, increased winter heating costs, and summer energy savings)[2]

13% — The percentage by which urban heat islands have increased the cooling load for a typical urban building[3]

80% TO 90% — The amount of sunlight absorbed by dark paving material[4]

50°F TO 60°F — The amount by which cool roofing materials can be cooler than traditional materials[5]

30°F TO 40°F — The amount by which a green roof can be cooler than conventional rooftops[6]

6.2 YEARS — The average payback time for installing a green roof on commercial and public buildings[7]

35°F — The maximum amount by which trees reduce surface temperatures; trees also reduce summer air temperatures 2° to 9°F in their vicinity[8]

10% — The decrease in office worker productivity in thermally uncomfortable and poorly ventilated environments[9]

SHUTTERSTOCK

Heat is already affecting the construction part of the real estate process because of worker safety concerns and material setting issues.

THE EMERGING BUSINESS CASE FOR ADDRESSING EXTREME HEAT

As extreme heat becomes increasingly prevalent because of the urban heat island effect and climate change, designing for heat and ensuring users' comfort is likely to become a mainstream concern. This translates into different design and development decisions for buildings, which may need enhanced cooling capacity, and for public spaces and outdoor retail environments that are likely to be used differently in hot weather.

Some developers are already acting. For example, LandSec, the largest property developer by assets in the historically temperate United Kingdom, has studied the likely physical impacts of climate change on its portfolio, noting the U.K.'s projected temperature increase.

"Life will be very different in our new, more extreme climate, and we can't create a product that doesn't perform," explains Edward Dixon, director of sustainability insights at LandSec. "For example, for the build-to-rent sector, if apartments are too hot to rent during the summer, customers will vote with their feet and leave. Climate resilience is critical to quality of product and will affect the competitiveness of every business in our sector."

As temperatures rise, developments that plan for extreme heat may gain a competitive advantage, whereas developments that are not prepared may incur costs, for the following reasons.

CONSUMER PREFERENCE: Without intervention, extreme heat can be a stressor, reducing retail sales at outdoor malls, changing recreation and travel choices, and otherwise influencing consumer behavior. Buildings and developments designed to maintain comfortable temperatures are preferable to tenants, buyers, and retail consumers regularly experiencing extreme heat. Similarly, outdoor spaces that are designed to provide cooler environments may have enhanced use and foot traffic. For outdoor retail and walkable transit-oriented-development neighborhoods, this traffic usually translates into improved sales, branding, and visibility.

> We're looking at heat mitigation to make the pedestrian experience comfortable.... Heat mitigation is a way to make sure that when people look at Sundance, they notice something special.
>
> JOHNNY CAMPBELL
> CEO, Sundance Square

BENEFITS OF HEAT RESILIENCE IN REAL ESTATE DEVELOPMENT

PROJECT DEVELOPMENT	PROJECT MARKETING	PROJECT COMPLETION	PROJECT OPERATIONS
• Reduced construction costs and reduced likelihood of construction delays caused by extreme heat • Faster permitting and increased buy-in from influential stakeholders, including investors, public officials, and community groups • Reduced stress on public infrastructure, potentially helping sustain long-term economic vibrancy and climate resilience in the local area	• Enhance project branding or boost a firm's reputation through high-quality, resilient design • Capture market demand for "green" building with extreme heat resilience as a differentiator • Public recognition through awards or iconic features	• Increased occupant comfort, site visitation, and/or retail sales when property is available as a cool place of refuge during normal hot-weather months and extreme heat events • Enhanced asset value, higher rent premiums, lower vacancy rates, or faster lease-up because of increased occupant comfort and/or likely increased productivity of building occupants	• Sustained value from avoidance of additional costs replacing heat-damaged materials, upgrading per regulatory requirements, and/or adding additional amenities per consumer demand • Long-term utility cost savings because of decreased cooling load and energy use, supporting an improved net operating income • Higher chance of sustained operations (business continuity) and occupant health during extreme heat events

Extreme heat resilience strategies can enhance revenue with "cool" amenities. For example, Hilton hired TBG Landscape Architects to redesign an outdoor pool and lounge area at its luxury Anatole Hotel in Dallas; TBG preserved shade trees, added light-colored materials to the pool to minimize heat absorption, installed built shade structures and umbrellas, and conducted a before-and-after study to assess the temperature change. The redesign created an inviting and comfortable amenity area that helped the hotel attract more clients and expand from a five-day-a-week business clientele to a seven-day-a-week business, family, and visitor establishment.

In locations where extreme heat is a growing concern, amenity expectations may shift. For example, consumer demand for air conditioning has recently become a factor in Seattle's competitive rental market; before the 2010s, only 6 percent of Seattle rentals had central air conditioning, but in response to rising temperatures, record apartment construction, and demand, that percentage has climbed to over 25 percent.[10]

BUILDING LONGEVITY, MAINTENANCE, AND OPERATIONS: High temperatures can directly damage building materials not selected to withstand extreme temperatures, thereby increasing rates of wear—especially for roofs—and accelerating deterioration. Similarly, extreme heat events can increase water use and stress vegetation, leading to landscape replacement costs. Buildings not equipped for longer, hotter summers or not designed for potential future policy changes may require renovations and retrofits or have a harder time attracting new tenants. In locations where climate change is expected to cause increased precipitation as well as heat, the combination of heat and humidity may increase mold and mildew issues, posing a health risk to tenants and increased expenses for owners or property managers.

Meaningful placemaking and an enjoyable user experience are common reasons designers and developers invest in heat-resilient design and amenities such as the Hilton Anatole's JadeWaters resort pool in Dallas.

ENERGY USE: As temperatures rise, buildings relying exclusively on air conditioning for cooling will experience higher energy costs. Such dependency also becomes a risk when electrical grid stability is compromised by extreme heat.

HVAC can constitute between 15 and 35 percent of a building's total energy demand (depending on climate and building use), and urban heat islands thus far have increased the typical cooling load of an urban building by an average of 13 percent.[11] For a commercial office building, where electricity and gas costs are typically $2 to $3 per square foot, a 13 percent reduction in HVAC (at 30 percent of building energy use) could yield savings of 8 to 12 cents per square foot.

Although heating costs may decrease in some locations, the "observed [nationwide] increase in cooling energy demand has been greater than the decrease in energy demand" since 1970.[12] If emissions are not reduced, energy expenses in Phoenix, for example, could increase by up to 9 percent by mid to late century, and Tucson could spend more than 1 percent of GDP annually on additional energy costs.[13]

> We're facing scenarios where summers are 5°F hotter with prolonged heat waves every other year.
>
> What types of properties will be attractive?
>
> Where will people want to live?
>
> What will be the effect on retail; how will people fill their leisure time?
>
> EDWARD DIXON
> Director, Sustainability Insights
> LandSec

Investing in strategies that support energy efficiency and indoor thermal comfort can have significant return on investment. Owner Henbart LLC partnered with a local university and a dynamic glass manufacturer to measure the impact of replacing single-paned windows with "intelligent" windows in a 1970s-era, 90,000-square-foot commercial office building in Seattle. Henbart measured energy costs, temperature, and tenant satisfaction and calculated a 17.7 percent decrease in building energy use leading to $28,000 in annual savings.[14]

BUSINESS CONTINUITY: Extreme heat can contribute to other adverse events such as electrical grid failures, transportation interruptions, wildfires, and water shortages, all of which can cause human harm, business disruptions, and economic losses. Buildings and developments designed to be more prepared for these events have the potential to be more attractive to tenants, particularly in class A office space, and may also eventually be eligible for preferable insurance rates. These types of weather-related continuity events also present risks because of potential property losses, tenant defaults, or both.[15]

LIABILITY: Extreme heat may increase the chances of lawsuits against developers and owners for system failures, degraded building materials, unstable operations, suffering tenants, and secondary impacts caused by buildings (such as melting parked car mirrors from reflected heat; see Melting Materials and Glare Damage, page 22). Even if owners are not found at fault, lawsuits are costly to resolve and a reputational risk. If more real estate professionals—especially in construction, architecture, design, and engineering—begin to consider extreme heat as part of their customary work process, the professional standards for successful, underperforming, or failed building could shift.

REGULATION: There are signs that regulatory measures may evolve to address extreme heat specifically, especially in markets where temperatures are rising and city officials are recognizing the contribution of buildings to the urban heat island effect. These regulations could lead to required building or site landscaping retrofits. To raise revenue for major heat-resilient infrastructure investments, cities may also consider measures (taxes, bonds, etc.), some of which could potentially increase business costs.

> We think green roofs cool rooftop decks by at least 10°F, if not more, in the hot summer months. The green roof makes the rooftop deck usable and a real amenity space.
>
> JAMES MARANSKY
> President, Ebuilt

LOONEY RICKS KISS ARCHITECTS/ULI

Deliberate efforts to prioritize efficient mechanical equipment to reduce long-term operating costs at Crosstown Concourse (Memphis, Tennessee), one of the world's largest historical adaptive use LEED Platinum buildings, paid off, achieving an energy cost savings of $1.3 million.

REGIONAL MARKET IMPACTS

Temperature—and available adaptation strategies—has historically been a driver in where people live and work in the United States. The summertime practice of fleeing hot inner cities for cooler rural surroundings is a common one (in contrast is the familiar phenomenon of retirees moving to or overwintering in warm states such as Arizona, California, and Florida). Once air conditioning became commonplace in the mid-20th century, growth rates increased significantly in some of the warmest parts of the country; the Sunbelt's share of the nation's population exploded from 28 percent in 1950 to 40 percent in 2000.[16]

OVER THE LONG TERM, EXTREME HEAT HAS THE POTENTIAL TO NEGATIVELY AFFECT ECONOMIC DEVELOPMENT, INFRASTRUCTURE, AND QUALITY OF LIFE IN SUSCEPTIBLE LOCATIONS, WHICH COULD ADVERSELY INFLUENCE THE GROWTH OF DIFFERENT REGIONAL REAL ESTATE MARKETS. Meanwhile, some locations with more temperate local climates may benefit.

Research has found that extreme temperatures are likely to be linked to a decrease in U.S. GDP through reduced growth rates and increased expenses. These trends are visible at the country, state, and city scales across sectors including finance, retail, and construction. By 2050, due to rising temperatures, median-sized U.S. cities can expect about a 1 percent loss in city GDP, assuming low future GHG emissions and slow rates of temperature increase, or as much as a 4 percent GDP loss by 2100, assuming no change in emissions and a significant increase in temperature.[17] One study based on the 1995 Chicago heat wave found that "Chicago's labor, maintenance, and capital investments would be 3.5 times higher under a high emissions scenario than under a low one" and that mean annual temperature and heat wave frequency were main drivers of those costs.[18]

GDP losses could affect cities' ability to raise capital (through taxes and municipal bonds) and the availability of capital for developers (as investors move to markets where heat impacts to their real estate investments are less severe or better mitigated by developers and cities). Likewise, if cities' credit ratings are downgraded, borrowing could become more expensive and real estate financing more difficult to secure, ultimately affecting project valuation.

As a community development corporation, we are trying to figure out how we deal with [heat], and there is no one formula. It is not just building stock, but also emergency preparedness and social cohesion.... How do you address this issue in an equitable way?

PHILIP GIFFEE
Executive Director, Neighborhood of Affordable Housing, a Boston-based community development corporation

MELTING MATERIALS AND GLARE DAMAGE

Some construction materials may not remain the best choices as climate zones shift, especially in historically temperate zones. For example, a 2018 summer heat wave was so hot in Scotland that rubber roofing material on Glasgow's Science Center "began melting, dripping black goo down the side of the building."[19]

Several years earlier, in London, a glass skyscraper in the heart of the financial district designed by the high-profile Rafael Vinoly Architects reflected so much heat onto the street below that it melted the wing mirrors and windshield wipers of nearby parked cars. In response, London suspended three parking bays in the area, and the building's developer paid for the vehicle damage.

High-cost fixes and reputation damage occur in the United States, too. The Walt Disney Concert Hall is Los Angeles is infamous for originally opening with so much glare that it caused automobile accidents before the exterior panels were dulled in 2005. In Dallas, the glare reflected from a 42-story luxury condominium development adjacent to the Nasher Sculpture Center damaged valuable art and became the subject of an episode in the television series *Engineering Catastrophes*.[20]

Building materials need to be carefully selected to withstand changing climate extremes.

In some markets, increased heat could put local infrastructure at risk and lead to significant broader economic impacts. For example, big tech firms are concerned about rising temperatures because of the resulting cost increase to cool their energy-intense data centers.[21] The impacts could also be especially significant for air travel (and the reliant business, logistics, and tourism sectors) because high temperatures interfere with airplanes' ability to take off. In July 2012, a US Airways plane at Washington, D.C.'s Reagan National Airport got stuck on the runway when tarmac softened from extreme heat;[22] similarly, the runways at New York's La Guardia Airport may become too short to allow planes to depart under worst-case-scenario temperature projections.[23]

Conversely, some U.S. regions that will not experience significant heat view temperature shifts as a potential opportunity. Cincinnati's 2018 sustainability plan, for example, has a section addressing the implications of being a "climate haven" for businesses and residents vacating more extreme climates, noting that the city will "cultivate its reputation as a safe location for risk averse businesses."[24] On an asset scale, climate havens could be buildings that act as cool spaces of refuge or provide services clients will want to access during extreme heat events.

High temperatures decrease the density of air, making it more difficult for planes to achieve the lift necessary for takeoff. To compensate, airlines can decrease the cargo weight, but under future worst-case-scenario climate projections, planes may need more runway distance to achieve the necessary lift.

AIR CONDITIONING IN FOCUS

Air conditioning (AC) can be a life-saving technology and is a standard amenity in most American real estate markets. However, the widespread use of air conditioning is problematic from a sustainability, energy consumption, and extreme heat standpoint. Air conditioning produces GHG emissions and waste heat, which (along with some types of AC refrigerant leakage) contribute to UHI formation and climate change.

Residential air conditioning is a critical health determinant during heat waves. It has reduced premature deaths in the United States on hot days by 75 percent since 1960, and most deaths during heat waves today occur in homes without AC.[25] Unfortunately, utility bills can be too expensive for some to afford to use their AC.

Today, over 90 percent of U.S. households have AC, but the distribution of air conditioning varies across geographic regions, demographics, and by the age of buildings.[26] "The people who are most at risk are the people who live without AC," observes Cincinnati's sustainability director, Larry Falkin. "My biggest concern is that in Cincinnati there are 13,000 housing units that do not have AC."

Residential air conditioning saves lives during extreme heat events, but access to air conditioning and the ability to afford higher utility costs is not equal across the United States.

MITIGATION AND ADAPTATION STRATEGIES

THERE IS NO "ONE SIZE FITS ALL" APPROACH TO EXTREME HEAT MANAGEMENT, but significant opportunity exists to design and build to alleviate urban heat effects and safeguard human health. Local conditions—especially humidity level—determine which mitigation and adaptation strategies will be effective and appropriate. The real estate sector can improve resilience to extreme heat through mitigation (strategies that directly reduce temperatures) as well as adaptation (actions that help people and businesses cope with or take advantage of the impacts of extreme heat). Developers are beginning to test emerging heat-mitigation technologies such as cool walls, reflective pavement, dynamic glass, and integrated solar photovoltaics.

WIDESPREAD ADOPTION OF TEMPERATURE REDUCTION STRATEGIES (I.E., MITIGATION) COULD POTENTIALLY REDUCE OR EVEN OFFSET THE URBAN WARMING TRENDS CURRENTLY OCCURRING IN CITIES, leaving them to contend with a more manageable 1° to 2°F background climate change increase, not the current 5° to 22°F urban heat island impact.[27] Adaptive strategies such as installing air conditioning and freely available drinking-water stations or implementing public education campaigns can encourage personal well-being.

SAMIA BYRD/ULI

A $30 million, 150,000-square-foot ribbon of steel, fabric, and glass covers the luxury retail space in Miami's Brickell City Center, creating a cooling effect and enjoyable shopping environment by preventing heat gain and redirecting breezes through the site.

DATA-DRIVEN HEAT MITIGATION

SITE ANALYSIS

Site analysis for heat mitigation includes collecting microclimate data in all seasons for geolocation, temperature, humidity, solar radiation, and wind direction and speed. Ecologists survey vegetation, tree canopy, water, and soils, typically by defining and analyzing small sample areas. At Sasaki, we model thermal comfort, including the surrounding environment and building massing, to calculate the existing baseline condition. Model variables include solar exposure, shadows, sky view, and wind in all seasons and times of day.

CONCEPT DESIGN

Site-responsive concept designs identify challenges and opportunities for heat mitigation and include building massing and entries, paths and streets, and intensive and extensive landscaped areas. The results from software analyses and climate consultants often suggest optimized architectural changes to building orientation, massing, or entry to increase thermal comfort in outdoor open spaces, paths, and streets. The results drive the locations for shading elements, seating areas, transportation hubs, and mechanical equipment or exhausts.

POSTOCCUPANCY EVALUATION

Site measurements verify the effect of the mitigation strategies. Ecologists return to sites to document biodiversity, water, and soil quality improvement. Self-verification or independent, third-party verification can also confirm outdoor thermal comfort metrics such as temperature, humidity, shade cover, and ecological quality.

NEXT STEPS

We can expand our work and research by designing for a 50- to 100-year project lifespan and changing climate. New tools project future as well as current weather data so our projects can continue to mitigate heat and respond to future climate impacts.

TAMAR WARBURG
Director of Sustainability, Sasaki Associates Inc.

FUTURE-PROOFING REAL ESTATE

Understanding climate risk and its real estate investment implications is a complex challenge for property investors. ULI's 2019 report in partnership with the global real estate investment manager Heitman, *Climate Risk and Real Estate Investment Decision-Making,* examines the physical and transitional risks associated with climate change and how investors are improving climate risk pricing and decision-making. Extreme heat was a topic that some investors raised in interviews for the project, noting the potential impacts of extreme heat on local economies and infrastructure function.

Forward-thinking firms are using natural catastrophe indices and analytical mapping exercises to understand the exposure and vulnerability of assets across their portfolios. Heat stress, drought, and wildfires are physical risks included in these assessments. Heat-related transitional risks are likely to be location-specific as local regulators consider policy solutions or transitional risks potentially related to the failure to adopt new heat-mitigation technologies. Read more at uli.org/futureproofingre.

HEAT ISLAND MITIGATION STRATEGIES (DISTRICT SCALE)

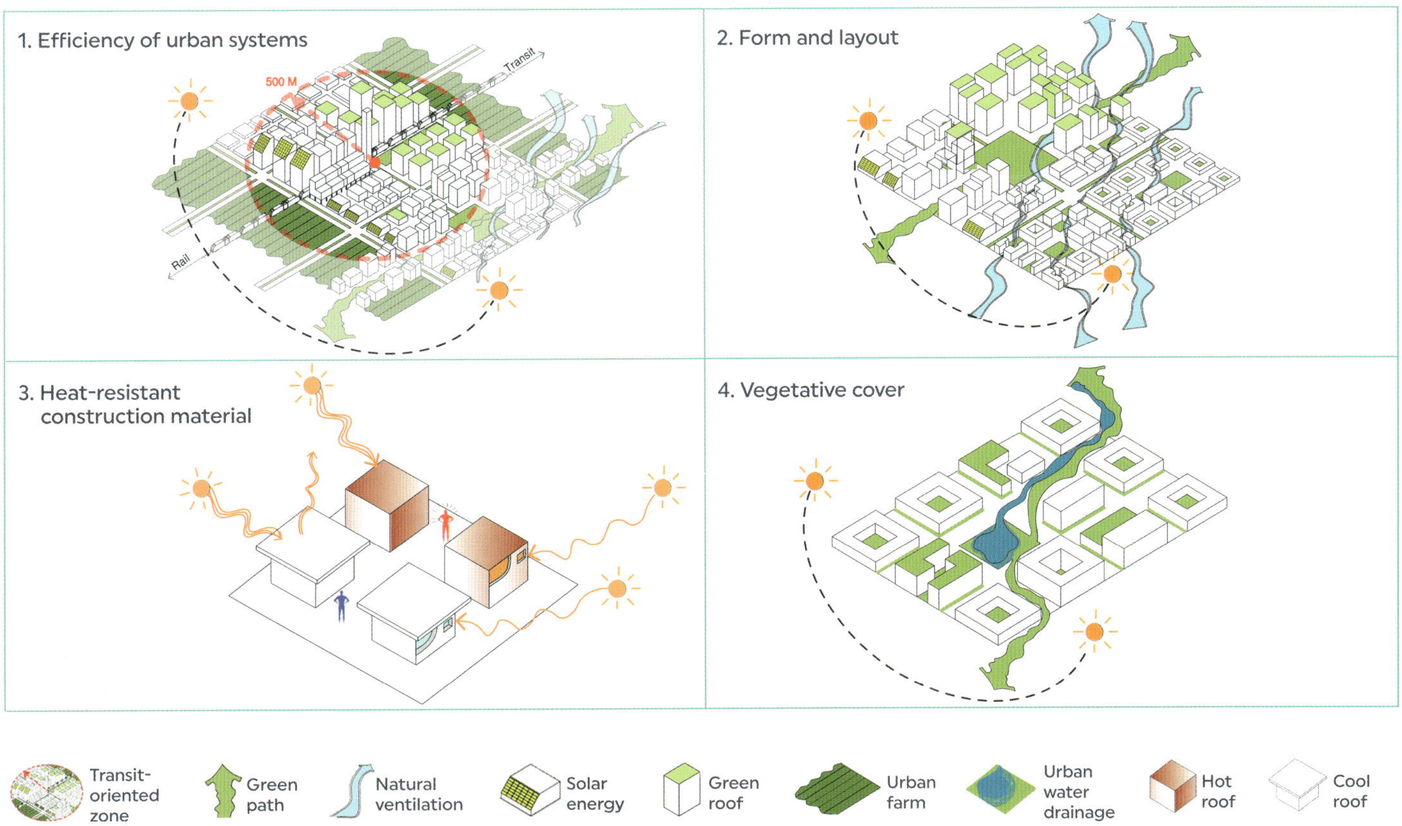

Four factors (waste heat and GHG emissions reduction, form and layout, heat-resistant building characteristics, and vegetative coverage) contribute to urban climate and are the backbone of holistic UHI mitigation efforts. (Jeffrey Raven, 2016; ULI NYC)

Shade Creation and Open Space

THE MOST UNIVERSALLY APPLICABLE RESILIENCE DESIGN STRATEGIES TO COMBAT EXTREME HEAT ARE THE CREATION OF SHADE AND THE PRESERVATION OF OPEN SPACE. No matter the local climate, shade provides welcome relief for pedestrians and reduces heat gain and cooling costs for buildings. In water-scarce regions where vegetation is often not the optimal shade strategy, built coverings provide benefits without adding to water demand. Similarly, parks and open spaces create cool green space islands that reduce surrounding air temperatures by at least (and sometimes far more than) 2° to 4°F and serve as places of refuge.[28]

"It's about how we plan our land to help reduce urban heat," elaborates Maritza Pechin, an urban planner with AECOM recently focused on master planning in Richmond, Virginia, "and that means parks, open spaces, and trees where they're needed most."

Other strategies address building mass, improve construction material selection, and lighten surface characteristics; minimize waste heat; and adopt district or site form and layout best practices. Green infrastructure—a broad category of strategies that decrease hardscapes and manage stormwater through natural systems approaches—often contributes to UHI mitigation. A 10 percent citywide increase in surface reflectivity and vegetation, for example, could reduce heat wave deaths by 6 to 7 percent.[29]

Effective implementation of emerging strategies requires thoughtful materials selection and sometimes tradeoffs. Cool surfaces, for example, successfully prevent heat absorption as compared to traditional dark surfaces but may inadvertently reflect that heat onto nearby pedestrians or buildings; the degree of reflectivity and the location of starkly light-colored materials (rooftop, building wall, sidewalk, etc.) are important design considerations.[30]

PEDESTRIAN THERMAL COMFORT EXPERIENCE

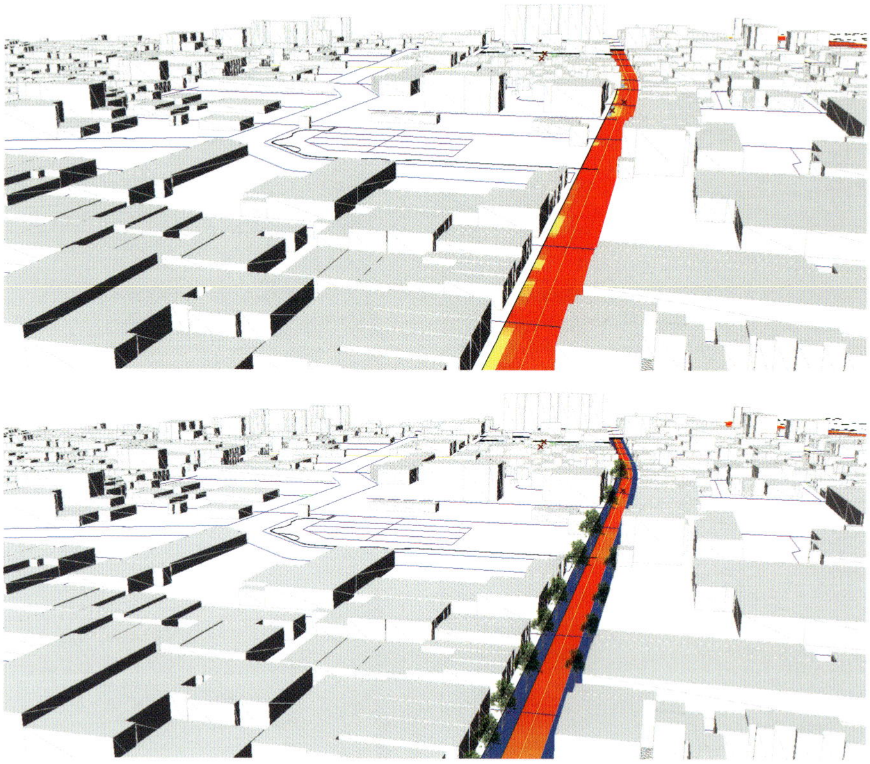

The diagram illustrates the thermal comfort difference pedestrians would experience traveling along an unshaded street and a 35 percent shaded street. (Anna Shenger Dai, NYIT Urban Design Climate Lab 2018)

In partnership with the Sacramento Tree Foundation, the Sacramento Municipal Utility District provides free shade trees and expert advice to customers, particularly those with low incomes or limited access to air conditioning.

Less heat-absorptive light-colored pavement, shade from the tree canopy, and evaporation from the vegetation create a thermally comfortable and inviting pedestrian environment. Such heat-conscious spaces contribute to a citywide increase in surface reflectivity and vegetation, which often measurably reduces heat wave deaths.

COOLING THE HEAT ISLAND EFFECT

CALCULATIONS BASED ON A 90-DEGREE DAY

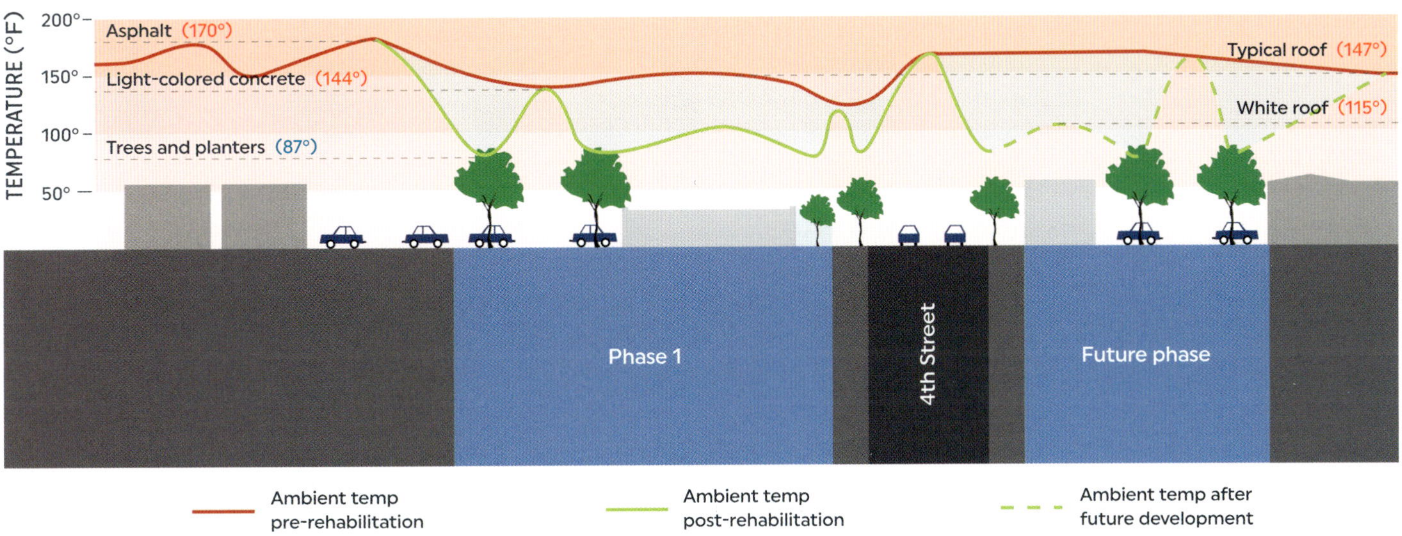

Temperature modeling for a redesigned development in Southern California estimates the cooler microclimates created by selecting white roofs and light-colored concrete as well as planting additional trees. (Studio One Eleven)

The project team for Meander Bend Park (an 18-acre space in Tucson, shown here before its redesign) created a cost/benefit analysis to calculate the social, environmental, and economic benefits of incorporating UHI mitigation features; the calculations returned an estimated UHI mitigation net present value of $1.8 million over 50 years. Read more at developingresilience.uli.org.

> Local temperature impacts are observable and measurable at the site scale.
>
> BARBARA DEUTSCH
> CEO, Landscape Architecture Foundation

Forward-Looking Climate Data

Because the climate is changing, some developers and designers are proactively working with future heat projections to anticipate future temperatures for the lifetime of a new building or development. "To design for yesterday's temperature is not our only responsibility; we need to design for the future as well," explains Tamar Warburg, director of sustainability at design firm Sasaki.

Alex Ramirez, a landscape architect with Design Workshop, emphasizes that conversations about future heat scenarios are becoming less unusual in discussions with city officials and developers. "Knowing the climate is changing [is] important for making these human environments more comfortable," he says. "We talk about human comfort a lot—especially in walkable neighborhoods. That trend has caught on, and it's an easier conversation to have now."

For some types of land uses, including utilities and infrastructure, understanding future heat projections is critical to determine whether existing systems will be able to continue to function. Firms specializing in climate data analytics are responding to this need, providing mapping that details projected temperatures. "Utilities, enterprises, and financial services firms are using extreme heat data to optimize infrastructure and other investments to reduce operations and maintenance costs and cool the environment," explains Rich Sorkin, the CEO of analytics firm Jupiter Intelligence.

However, using future climate projections for building energy modeling and to guide design remains a new and occasionally controversial approach. Especially for large commercial developments, implementing mitigation measures to account for climate conditions in 2050 and beyond can significantly increase project costs. Some developers are also concerned about the difficulty of sourcing heat-mitigation technologies in a cost-effective and timely manner because of the sometimes limited production of cutting-edge technologies.

SPORTS STADIUMS AND OLYMPICS STRATEGIC PLANNING

Extreme heat is a major consideration for sports infrastructure. In January 2018, architectural design firms Populous and Gould Evans were jointly awarded the opportunity to design a new major league soccer stadium for Phoenix Rising in part because of their heat-aware proposal. "We need to build a stadium that will be comfortable for both the fans and players, so it was crucial that the winning architectural design team understood the challenges and opportunities associated with the Sonoran Desert," said Brett Johnson, co-chairman for Phoenix Rising, in the press release announcing the decision.[31]

Sports infrastructure can also be controversial. Citing gender discrimination and safety concerns (including burns), the U.S. Women's National Team campaigned extensively against artificial turf fields during the 2015 soccer World Cup. While the less competitive men's team played on grass, the turf field for the women's opening match in Canada that year was 120°F at kickoff when the air temperature was 75°F.[32]

Similarly, the planning team for the 2020 Tokyo Olympics (July 24–August 9) is making numerous adjustments because of anticipated heat and humidity, including installing misting stations, placing shade tents over security lines, shifting competition start times to cooler morning hours, and installing reflective paving over the 26.2-mile marathon racecourse.

SHUTTERSTOCK

In competitive sports, extreme heat is literally a game changer when it impacts competitors' health and fans' experience at live events; over 30 sports stadiums worldwide are LEED-certified, and heat mitigation and adaptation are increasingly common factors in newer U.S. stadiums.

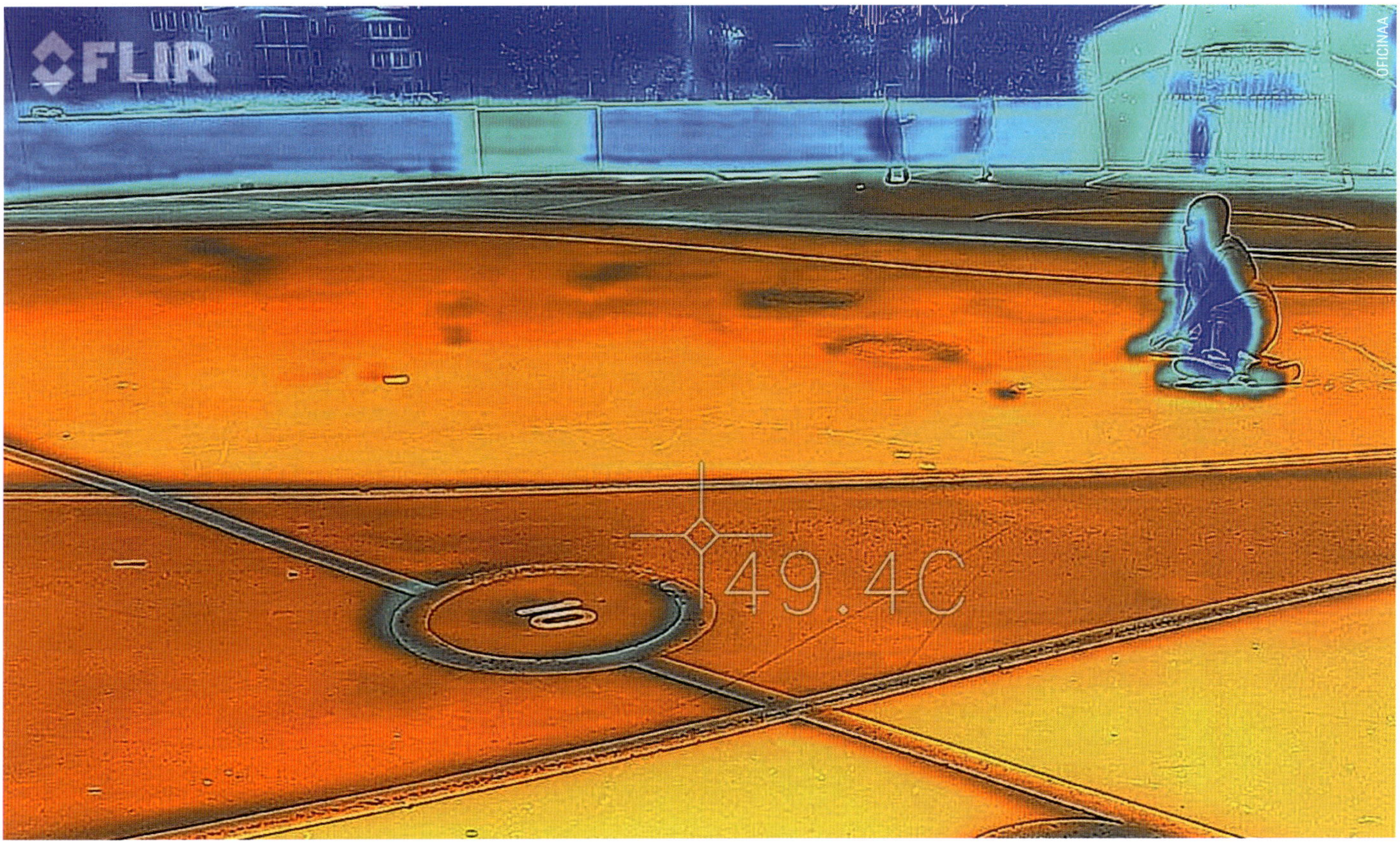

OFICINAA

Thermal imaging of a playground in Cambridge, Massachusetts, shows that the dark color of the ground material and lack of shade have raised surface temperatures to 49.4°C (120.92°F), which will create stress on the child who is still cool from being in an air-conditioned building.

OVERVIEW OF MITIGATION AND ADAPTATION STRATEGIES: BUILDINGS AND SITES

STRATEGY	DESCRIPTION
BUILDING DESIGN	
Orientation	The strategic orientation of a building, doors, and windows helps minimize solar heat gain and optimize ventilation. Typically, buildings are oriented north–south to reduce sun exposure, and windows are oriented toward the prevailing winds to maximize cross breezes.[33]
Shape	A building's shape can provide shade—and thus cooling—to other parts of the structure and to surrounding pedestrian environments. A courtyard design with buildings oriented around a small central plaza is a typical hot-climate strategy that minimizes outside heat gain by creating an internal shaded area.
Massing	Heavy, dense materials with high thermal mass (the ability of a material to store and release heat) can keep a building cool and modulate temperature swings. Materials such as concrete, tiles, brick, and stone absorb daytime heat and release it slowly at night if and when the temperature drops.[34]
BUILDING MATERIALS AND ENGINEERING	
Building envelopes	Building envelopes, the physical barrier between the internal and external environments providing structural support, moisture management, air flow, and temperature regulation, are one of the most important and challenging aspects of heat mitigation through building design.[35] High-quality insulation and certain materials can prevent solar heat gain into and encourage the efficient heat dissipation out of buildings.[36] Windows, if they are operable, glazed, or shaded, are a key component; windows leverage natural airflow to increase human comfort and decrease HVAC load.
Shading structures	A variety of impactful, often cost-effective structures, either permanent or temporary, can be installed on a building or as part of landscape design. Examples include awnings or umbrellas over windows or streets and structures covered with shading vegetation.
Waste heat reduction	Waste heat management is generally accomplished by reducing building cooling load (i.e., the waste heat generated by electrical equipment, lights, and people) and creating alternative outlets for rejecting heat rather than venting it directly on the street. Electric and ground-source heat pumps or heat recovery chillers can be used to move waste heat from a location where it is not wanted (such as an office space) to a location where it is needed (such as heating of domestic hot water) or stored for use during the winter months. Recycling heat in this way improves the efficiency of the cooling system and results in less heat rejection to the urban environment.
HVAC	Efficient HVAC systems safeguard human well-being by regulating indoor temperatures, keeping energy demand and costs low, and minimizing environmental impact. Industry standard equipment includes the Consortium for Energy Efficiency, Energy Star, and FEMP-designated certifications. Solar thermal water heaters are especially useful in extreme environments because they avoid the need for a boiler.
Lighting	Inefficient lighting adds to a building's heat load. Switching to LEDs and using strategies such as daylight dimming and occupancy-based lighting reduce the building's energy use and heating load.
Sensors and smart buildings	Sensors (temperature, occupancy, daylighting, motion, and carbon dioxide) enable automatic monitoring and adjustments, thus increasing energy efficiency.

STRATEGY	DESCRIPTION
LIGHT-COLORED AND REFLECTIVE SURFACES	
Cool roofs	By reflecting more sunlight and absorbing less heat, cool roofs are typically 50° to 60°F cooler than standard roofs during peak summer heat and, on average, produce energy savings of 20 percent.[37] Cool roofs are made of highly reflective paints, sheet coverings, or reflective shingles/tiles. Traditionally bright white, products can now meet demand for other colors without sacrificing cooling.
Cool walls	Cool walls use an exterior wall surface that stays cool by reflecting sunlight and emitting heat. They are not a widespread technology in the United States but have considerable potential because cool walls effectively cool building interiors and surrounding temperature.
Cool pavements	Cool pavements are light colored, reflective, or porous and work respectively via increased reflectance and/or heat-dissipating evaporation. There are many types, including light-colored and/or permeable coatings, aggregates, cement, and block pavement filled with materials such as soil, vegetation, or gravel. An emerging technology, life-cycle analysis of reflective paving has demonstrated energy, carbon, and cost concerns.[38] Additionally, reflective pavement may reflect heat onto pedestrians and nearby buildings. Many ongoing reflective paving pilot projects and material development research initiatives exist.[39]

We did over 100,000 energy building simulations across the U.S. and found that the energy savings from cool walls are generally equal to or greater than that of cool roofs.

RONNEN LEVINSON, Director, Heat Research Group of Lawrence Berkeley National Laboratory

STRATEGY	DESCRIPTION
GREEN INFRASTRUCTURE	
Green roofs	A "green" or "living," "vegetated," or "eco" roof is one that is wholly or partially covered by vegetation planted over a waterproof membrane. There are three main categories: extensive, intensive (the most effective for heat mitigation), and semi-intensive. Green roofs are a high-impact temperature reduction strategy with multiple co-benefits and often local government incentives. However, their success depends on local conditions, and they may not be appropriate for arid locations due to water constraints.
Green walls	"Green" walls or "vertical landscaping" is composed of plants grown in vertical systems along interior or exterior walls. Green walls can be extensive ("green facades") or intensive ("living walls"). Green walls are an attractive amenity, reduce building energy use, and decrease building envelope surface temperatures as well as surrounding microclimate temperatures. Similar to other vegetative strategies, "the cooling effect of green walls is highly dependent on their orientation, plant density and water content."[40]
OPERATIONAL CHANGES	
Thermostat control	Strategically setting and/or adjusting thermostats maximizes energy efficiency and can contribute to reduced energy grid demand. Some New York City public offices, for example, decrease air conditioning use on high-demand days to lesson peak demand and schedule demonstration days without air conditioning.
Schedule modifications	Adjusting working or school hours to minimize people's exposure to heat (i.e., time outdoors in extreme conditions or in places without air conditioning) is a common strategy for the approximately 50 percent of U.S. classrooms without any or adequate air conditioning.[41]

OVERVIEW OF MITIGATION AND ADAPTATION STRATEGIES: DISTRICT SCALE

CATEGORY	DESCRIPTION
URBAN DEVELOPMENT PATTERNS	
Urban geometry and density	Urban heat islands are more significant in cities arranged in geometric, gridlike patterns because of the way that heat reradiated off buildings is absorbed by other buildings that face them directly.[42] Cities that are large (in land area and population) and densely developed usually have more significant heat islands than smaller, more sprawling, and less dense cities. However, higher-density cities also offer important opportunities for sustainable and energy-efficient living, such as transit and higher-density residential development. Density, if implemented with extreme heat resilient best practices, can achieve sustainability and quality-of-life benefits while also mitigating the urban heat island effect.[43]
Waste heat reduction	Implementing efficient urban systems that reduce or eliminate waste heat diffusion into the local environment can reduce the urban heat island effect and GHG emissions (the root of rising temperatures from climate change). Strategies that support energy efficiency across industries and lead to increased public transit use and decreased vehicle miles traveled will contribute positively to reducing waste heat. Similarly, district energy systems can help mitigate UHIE by consolidating heat rejection for a neighborhood into one location (ideally away from major public and residential spaces) where that concentrated waste heat can be used for district heating or electrical generation.
Ventilation corridors	A factor of urban design as well as local topographical and meteorological conditions, the movement of air through a city or building helps dissipate heat and (within a reasonable velocity) increase human comfort. Varied building forms encourage airflow and ventilation, which can also be influenced by other factors, including road orientation relative to prevailing winds, building density, aspect ratio, and sky view factor.
Parks and open spaces	Parks (and their associated vegetation and lack of dark, impervious surfaces) create "cool park islands" that reduce surrounding air temperatures and provide a healthier, more comfortable place of refuge. The preservation, orientation, and design of open spaces can also be optimized to contribute to ventilation corridors.
Urban canopy	Trees and other vegetation cool temperatures through shade (reducing solar radiation and its reflection onto nearby buildings) and evapotranspiration (dissipating heat).[44] Many experts refer to trees as the "cheapest beneficial infrastructure." Trees reduce summer air temperatures in their vicinity by 2° to 9°F and surface temperatures by as much as 35°F.[45]
Water features	Adding water features or preserving naturally occurring systems can be a highly effective cooling strategy at multiple scales. However, water features can also absorb large amounts of daytime heat and reradiate it at night. In humid locations, water features can raise humidity and therefore the temperature "real feel." Water systems are most effective in locations with dry (not humid) air and significant air movement.

MORRIS MALAKOF

Water features, such as these orange fountains in Houston's Levy Park, are an effective cool design strategy in dry climates but sometimes not effective in locations where humidity is a significant concern.

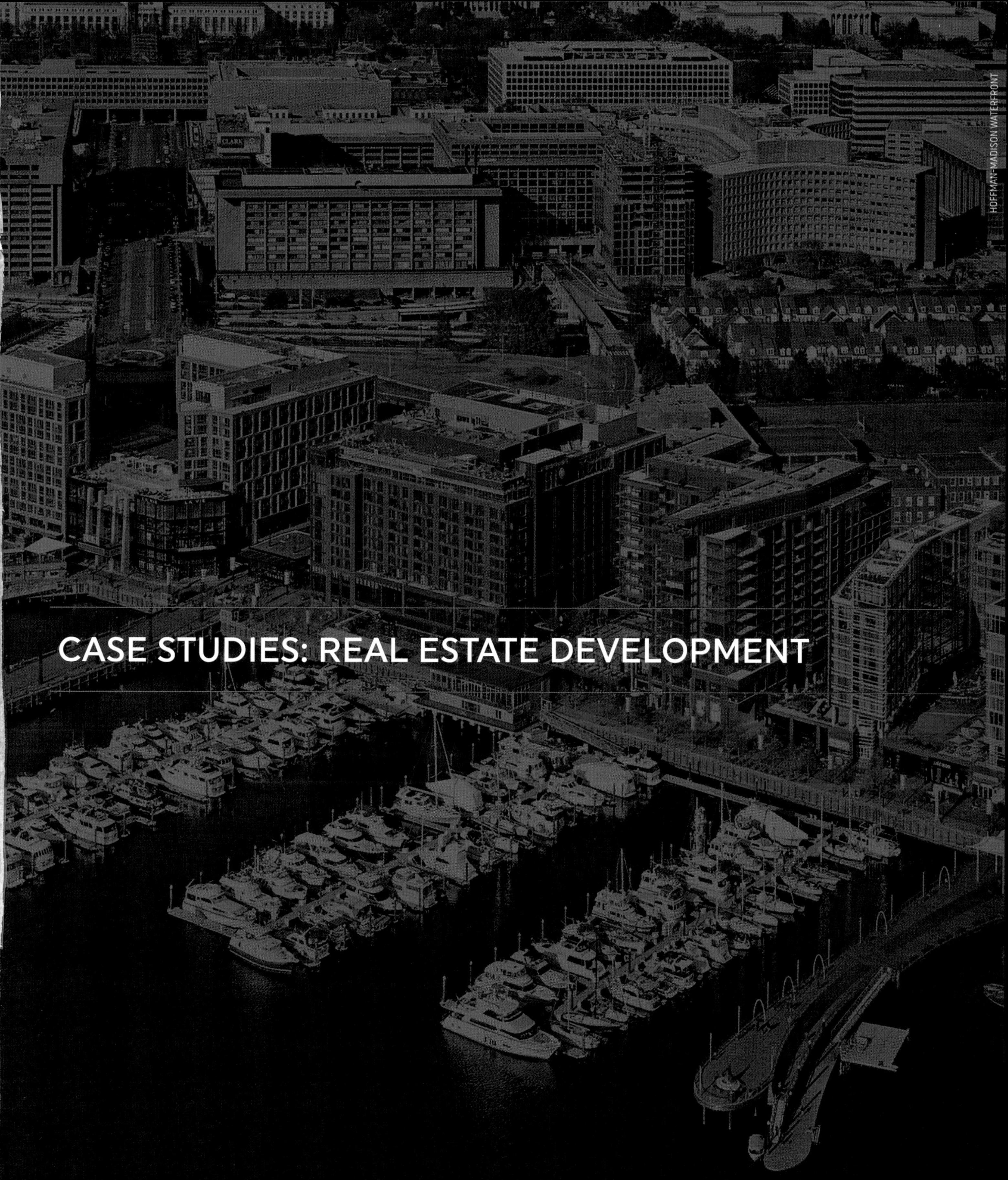

HOFFMAN-MADISON WATERFRONT

CASE STUDIES: REAL ESTATE DEVELOPMENT

Leading real estate professionals are incorporating heat-resilient building and infrastructure designs and, as a result, are noticing lower operations and management costs, regional recognition and fast lease-up rates, and improved tenant and occupant experience.

STREETSCAPE

HOUSTON, TEXAS

BAGBY STREET

DEVELOPMENT TEAM:
Houston Midtown Redevelopment Authority, Design Workshop, SER Construction Partners

EXTREME HEAT MANAGEMENT FEATURES:
Shade trees, heat- and drought-resilient landscaping, light-colored pavement

YEAR CONSTRUCTED:	SIZE:	COST:
2013	13 blocks, 0.62 miles	$13 million

In Houston, the reconstruction of a main corridor called Bagby Street with extreme heat and flood mitigation measures has contributed to a positive community environment, increased development opportunities, and earned the neighborhood widespread recognition. Bagby Street, originally a four-lane throughway, is located in a tax reinvestment zone in Midtown Houston, a central neighborhood just south of the downtown core that has experienced significant growth since the early 2010s.

With that growth and increased demand on public infrastructure and utilities, the Bagby Street corridor was in need of major repairs and upgrades, especially to its stormwater infrastructure. "We saw it as an opportunity," says Marlon Marshall, director of engineering and construction for the Midtown Redevelopment Authority (MRA), "to develop a sustainable capital improvement project to try to induce additional development in this area."

Mitigating the urban heat island to ensure pedestrian comfort was a central design strategy; hot temperatures in Houston are a concern six months of the year from May to October. The project team also wanted to improve stormwater management to be prepared for Houston's occasional heavy rains and hurricanes.

Before the reconstruction, 10 of Bagby Street's 13 sidewalk blocks were in disrepair, and commuters used it primarily as a cut-through to reach two nearby highways. In addition, Bagby Street required significant drainage and utility updates, and averaged a summer surface temperature of 108°F.

Bagby Street has been reconstructed to provide more public space, attract development, and remain comfortable, walkable, and usable during times of extreme heat and flooding.

> We put Bagby Street on a "road diet" and gave a bunch of space back to the public.
>
> ALEX RAMIREZ
> Associate, Design Workshop

DESIGN WORKSHOP

The absence of utility poles on one side of Bagby Street is an intentional strategy to eliminate overhead conflicts with big, effective shade trees and reduce maintenance costs.

EXTREME HEAT RESILIENCE STRATEGIES

To meet the Midtown Redevelopment Authority's goals, landscape architect and urban planning firm Design Workshop proposed reducing Bagby Street from four to two lanes, incorporating pedestrian safety features, and adding significant green infrastructure. Downsizing the road allowed a 38 percent increase in seating and social gathering space, which has contributed to "increased pedestrian activity," says Marshall. To support the increased pedestrian traffic, Design Workshop used heat-resistant paving materials and landscaping to maintain a comfortable environment. The firm selected pavers with a high solar reflectance value and 25 percent recycled material content. "The pavers cost about double what concrete would generally cost," says Ramirez, "but they contribute to the branding and identity the Midtown District desired."

The extra space allowed the addition of 175 new large shade trees along the corridor, which would also reduce temperature and improve the pedestrian environment. The redesign also included rain gardens with heat- and drought-tolerant plant species and aligned new permanent irrigation infrastructure with a small park adjacent to the street.

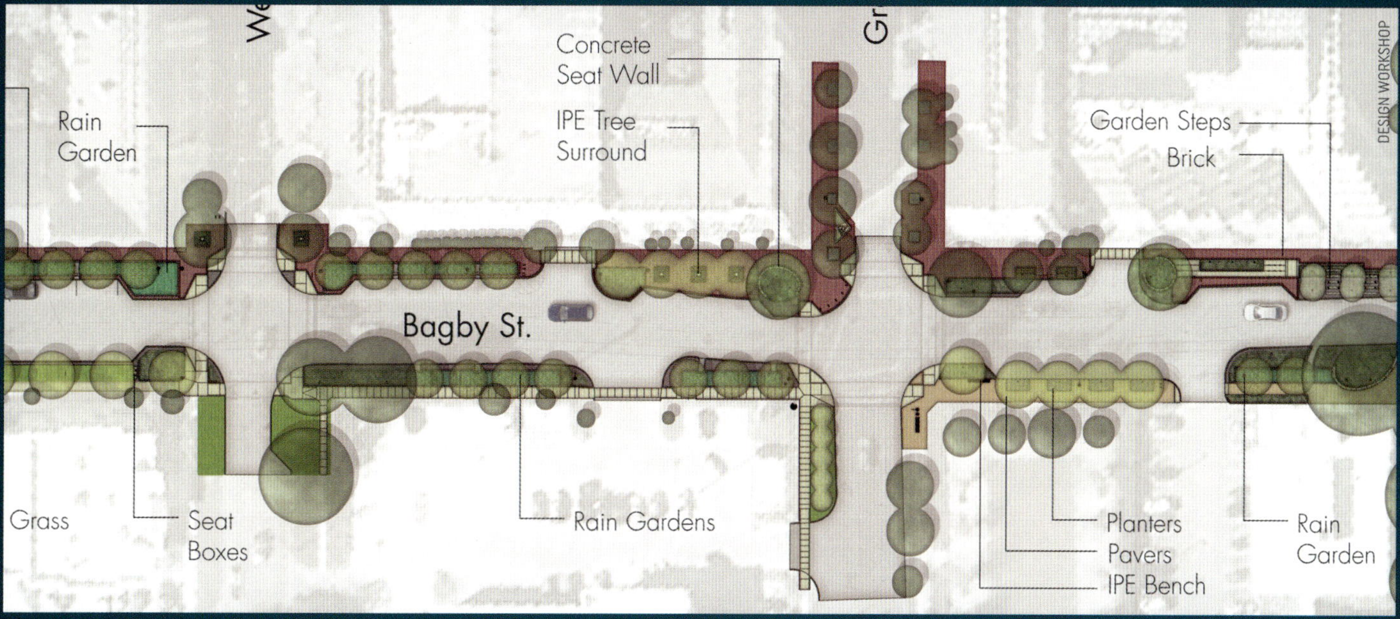

The master plan for Bagby Street added 175 new large shade trees to provide 90 percent shade coverage along the corridor, achieving a 20°F reduction in the shaded areas.

OUTCOME

The corridor's new design has significantly improved local business, pedestrian experience, and environmental outcomes, earning its place as the first Greenroads-certified project in Texas and the highest-scoring Greenroads project for several years until 2017 when the Sellwood Bridge in Oregon surpassed Bagby Street by one point in the rating system.[46] Bagby Street has also received recognition from the American Society of Landscape Architects, the American Council of Engineering Companies, and the Congress for the New Urbanism.[47]

Moreover, "we've shown that green infrastructure can be beneficial from a dollars and cents standpoint," says Marshall. In the first year after the reconstruction, nearly $30 million in private development was invested along Bagby Street. Property values along the street have increased 25 percent and 20 percent for the rental market. "Abandoned parcels were redeveloped into bars and restaurants," says Ramirez.

MRA and its partner organization Midtown Management District, responsible for operations and maintenance, have also realized cost savings and work efficiencies from the redesign. By aligning Bagby's irrigation infrastructure with the nearby park, for example, Midtown has seen a steady 10 percent water bill reduction every year since the reconstruction.

In addition to installing new heat-mitigation features and additional stormwater infrastructure, Design Workshop and MRA coordinated with the local utility providers to replace overhead utilities on taller poles and consolidate poles on one side of the street. Those changes eliminate half the street's overhead power-line conflicts with the big shade trees and allow the trees on the side of the street with utility lines to grow larger before needing to be trimmed, thereby reducing maintenance costs.

> Bagby Street has become a significant node of attractive establishments. It's been very successful over the last four to five years.
>
> MARLON MARSHALL
> Director of Engineering and Construction
> Midtown Redevelopment Authority

"Bagby has become a model project," says Marshall. "We've had national visitors and presented it at many conferences as a prototype of tackling a number of aspects, including human comfort from a heat perspective."

Design Workshop used a heat gun to measure surface temperatures at the street level; "there's about a 20-degree Fahrenheit difference between areas where the direct sunlight is hitting pavement to pavement in the shade," says Ramirez. The new design achieved a 42 percent increase in shade on sidewalks, allowing 90 percent total shade coverage and a 14 percent reduction in surface temperatures throughout the corridor.

The green infrastructure is also an asset during times of heavy rains and hurricanes. Since completion, Bagby has weathered three major flood events, including Hurricane Harvey (2017). "While many other areas of Midtown Houston flooded," says Marshall, "there was no flooding on Bagby Street during any of those major flood events. We're proud of how Bagby performed."

AFFORDABLE HOUSING, MIXED USE, PARK

PHOENIX, ARIZONA

EDISON EASTLAKE

DEVELOPMENT TEAM:
City of Phoenix Housing Department, Mithun Inc., Gorman & Company, Arizona State University

EXTREME HEAT MANAGEMENT FEATURES:
Building orientation and materials, open space, tree canopy, shade structures, cooling centers, emergency management planning

YEAR CONSTRUCTED:	SIZE:	COST:
Under development	1,161 units, 9.83 acres	$220 million

The city of Phoenix's Housing Department is advancing a strategy to redevelop Edison Eastlake as a heat-resilient, affordable neighborhood east of downtown. Supported by a $1.5 million U.S. Department of Housing and Urban Development (HUD) Choice Neighborhood Planning and Action Grant and $193 million from the city, the project will redevelop 557 outdated public housing units into a mixed-income community of more than 1,000 new homes to be heat resilient and more walkable, healthier, and connected. The Edison Eastlake One Vision Plan, led by design firm Mithun and created with residents and stakeholders, lays out the strategy for redevelopment and identifies cooling the urban heat island effect as one of three top implementation priorities.

The three public housing developments (Sidney P. Osborn Homes, A.L. Krohn Homes, and Frank Luke Homes) that make up the Edison Eastlake site were constructed between 1942 and 1963 and suffer from mold, failing systems, and an isolating design.[48]

Further, the neighborhood was subject to redlining in the 1930s and 1950s (preventing people of color from securing financing to buy homes), so current homeownership is low (16 percent in 2019).[49] The area has recently experienced high unemployment and crime rates, and more than 80 percent of local residents have annual incomes less than $11,000, making it one of the poorest areas in central Phoenix.[50]

Temperatures in Edison Eastlake are also among the hottest in Maricopa County.[51] Surface temperature maps from Arizona State University show that Edison Eastlake is on average 105°F during the summer and often 130°F on extreme days.[52] Moreover, unlike other areas in Phoenix, Edison Eastlake has low vehicle ownership, so residents are walking, biking, or taking public transportation and are "out there in the heat all summer long," says Cindy Stotler, director of the Phoenix Housing Department.

HEAT REDUCTION AND PRACTICAL RESILIENCE

SITE-SPECIFIC STRATEGIES

- Photovoltaics
- New ramada/shade structures
- New GRiD bike share station
- Community gardens/food hub
- Outdoor gathering space
- New play area
- New green space
- Shaded multi use trail
- 1 Thermal comfort pilot project
- 2 Storm water runnels + bioswales

Edison Eastlake's master plan proposes cooling the urban heat island effect with passive house design, shaded open green spaces and walkways, and cool paving and pilot-testing emerging technologies such as a cooling tower. (Mithun)

As part of the One Vision Plan, the city, supported by community organizations Local Initiatives Support Corporation–Phoenix and Vitalyst, conducted a two-year community feedback process that began with a detailed Health Impact Assessment survey. "One of the major findings of the Health Impact Assessment was that the urban heat island is significantly impacting the health of residents," says Stotler.

Residents identified heat-related health concerns, including respiratory and cardiovascular disease, specific heat illness, and lack of ability to walk safely, and supported the idea of "practical resilience through redevelopment."

EXTREME HEAT RESILIENCE STRATEGIES

Mithun developed new housing prototypes that seek to mitigate extreme heat by maximizing shade and ventilation and incorporating cool building materials. For example, courtyard housing maximizes shade, and single-loaded apartments with open breezeways on one side and apartments that have operable windows on both sides allow for cross ventilation.

Energy efficiency is another priority. "We go for as much energy efficiency as possible," says Stotler, "because we're building to own forever, don't have the money to rehab, and want to save residents on their utility bills."

The site plan also maximizes green space while taking an intentional approach to water efficiency. Clusters of drought-tolerant and native plants will provide cool islands, supplemented by strategic lawn areas. Planned public spaces and rights-of-way adhere to Phoenix's zoning code requirement that all new sidewalks must be 75 percent shaded. Cool paving technologies including experimental coatings and paving materials are being explored for paths and sidewalks.

The One Vision Plan includes emergency preparedness in its heat resilience approach; the planning team debated adding backup water supply and generators to each building but concluded a more doable method would be to include those elements in common facilities. Community meeting places, including a central festival street and cultural corridor, are provided in each block, creating "a logical meeting place for people who can't get very far to organize and help each other in a disaster," says Erin Christensen Ishizaki, partner at Mithun.

We are focused on bringing up the entire neighborhood to higher wealth, health, and education standards.

CINDY STOTLER
Director, Phoenix Housing Department

Custom housing prototypes with central courtyards, open breezeways, and operable windows help maximize shade, ventilation, and energy efficiency at Edison Eastlake.

OUTCOME

In 2018, Phoenix Housing won—through a very competitive process—an additional $30 million HUD Implementation Grant, the largest ever received in Arizona, using the One Vision Plan in the application. The Implementation Grant covers one-third to one-fifth the cost of the redevelopment; while financing is being finalized, Gorman Partners was selected by the city in July 2018 as the development partner.[53]

Plan implementation in Edison Eastlake is already underway. Phoenix Housing has begun development on one vacant lot, and construction for the first new housing development of 177 units is planned to begin January 2020. The project will be phased in over six years (the length of the Implementation Grant).

Building on the One Vision Plan, Phoenix Housing's staff are finalizing neighborhood and housing details, especially those factors, such as setbacks and window design, that relate to heat mitigation. Phoenix Housing also continues to coordinate with Arizona State University to track heat in the neighborhood and the success of UHI mitigation measures. Arizona State University researchers have installed multiple weather stations in the neighborhood to measure baseline temperatures and track neighborhood temperature change from construction through buildout.

MIXED USE

ARLINGTON, VIRGINIA

NATIONAL LANDING

DEVELOPMENT TEAM:
JBG Smith

EXTREME HEAT MANAGEMENT FEATURES:
Reflective paving, street trees, green roofs, parks and open space

YEAR CONSTRUCTED:
2018

SIZE:
17,000 sq ft

COST:
$40,000

At National Landing, the neighborhood that will soon host Amazon's famed Arlington headquarters site, heat and humidity are major issues for developer JBG Smith. Much of the area includes office development constructed in the 1960s and 1970s, featuring superblocks and expansive plazas, often without significant vegetation. To make the district more attractive to prospective tenants—Amazon and others—JBG Smith initiated a comprehensive placemaking plan to improve the area's streetscape, sidewalks, parks, and other outdoor gathering spaces in mid-2017.

To create this vibrant and climatically comfortable environment, JBG Smith is testing a reflective pavement sealant as an urban heat island mitigation strategy as well as installing additional trees, green space, and green roofs. Crystal City's climate action plan notes that "quality of life will be affected by increasing heat stress, . . . severe weather events, and reduced availability of insurance for at-risk properties."[54] Today, the region experiences 30 dangerously hot and humid days each year; however, climate projections indicate 30 to 45 more of these heat emergency days per year by 2050.[55]

Initiatives to improve sustainability and build resilience are critical to successfully accommodating continued growth in the region and enhancing the community's quality of life.

TRACY GABRIEL
President and Executive Director,
Crystal City Business Improvement District

Excluding Amazon's proposed land purchase, JBG Smith controls 7.4 million square feet of development opportunities and owns 6.2 million square feet of existing office space and 2,850 multifamily units in National Landing, which is located across the Potomac River from Washington, D.C., and comprises Crystal City, the eastern portion of Pentagon City, and Potomac Yard.[56]

The reflective paving pilot project is key to JBG Smith's efforts to enhance the pedestrian experience. In an interview for a local paper, JBG Smith's chief development officer, Brian Coultner, reported, "We're really excited about the possibility and potential of this. If this has the type of impact we're looking for . . . it will work well for the people who visit and the people who live there."[57]

JBG SMITH

Developer JBG Smith installed 550 gallons of reflective coating over 17,000 square feet and is evaluating the pilot project's outcomes as part of a placemaking strategy.

The newly defined National Landing neighborhood and planned home of Amazon HQ2 encompasses Crystal City, Pentagon City, and Potomac Yard in Northern Virginia, just across the Potomac River from Washington, D.C.

EXTREME HEAT RESILIENCE STRATEGIES

In October 2018, JBG Smith installed 550 gallons of reflective coating over 17,000 square feet in the core of the National Landing district.[58] The size of the National Landing site and the concentration of JBG Smith's holdings "provides an incredible opportunity to try new innovative technologies" says Bryan Moll, executive vice president of development. The test site is a private driveway between two office buildings (two of which will be occupied by Amazon) that will have low to moderate traffic.

> We were looking to incorporate a number of sustainable technologies throughout the district, and we knew reflective paving is a relatively new product on the East Coast.
>
> BRYAN MOLL
> Executive Vice President of Development, JBG Smith

The reflective sealant is a gray-colored, water-based asphalt emulsion sealcoat (a mix of asphalt cement with additional minerals, polymers, and emulsifiers; it is not a paint) designed to be 33 percent reflective. Typically, two coats are applied to ensure 100 percent coverage of the underlying asphalt. The reflective paving costs $2.40 per square foot, in addition to the underlying asphalt.

JBG Smith's pilot project costs are about $40,000, including installation. Installation of the sealant took about two weeks.

OUTCOME

JBG Smith plans to evaluate the impact of the pavement on local surface and air temperatures as well as on pedestrian experience during summer 2019. "We are going to be measuring how it stands up and how it measures in humid heat," explained Ayisha Swann, development associate with JBG Smith. The firm anticipates hiring a consultant to conduct temperature readings, considering both the magnitude of the impact adjacent to the installation and the geographic range of that effect. Engineers will also critique the product's durability through a visual assessment.

If the product is successful in mitigating temperature, JBG Smith anticipates continuing to test the product on other parts of the National Landing site with differing amounts of pedestrian and vehicular traffic. "The immediate next steps may be secondary streets, including private or semi-private streets," explained Moll. "If we end up finding that this product is everything we hoped for, the end game would be applying it to highly trafficked roads." A large-scale application would present opportunities for partnership with Arlington County, which owns most of the roads within National Landing.

Ultimately, urban heat island mitigation represents an important component of the placemaking, sustainability, and future development strategy for National Landing. Amazon is investing $2.5 billion in the area for its second headquarters, and $1.8 billion from state and local governments and nearby universities Virginia Tech and George Mason University will fund, among other initiatives, two new Metro entrances, a pedestrian bridge, and a commuter rail hub. The transit improvements are adjacent to JBG Smith's holdings.

MIXED USE

SCOTTSDALE, ARIZONA

SKYSONG

DEVELOPMENT TEAM:
Plaza Companies, Holualoa Companies, City of Scottsdale, Arizona State University Foundation, Butler Design Group

EXTREME HEAT MANAGEMENT FEATURES:
Building orientation and siting, efficient facade, vegetative and built shade, energy-efficient lighting and HVAC

YEAR CONSTRUCTED:
2006, ongoing

SIZE:
42 acres

COST:
$300,000,000

SkySong, the ASU Scottsdale Innovation Center, is a high-profile mixed-use development where responsible planning has resulted in heat-conscious site layout, building design, and landscaping that help attract tenants and reflect the founding partners' forward-thinking, entrepreneurial vision.

SkySong is a partnership between Arizona State University Foundation, the city of Scottsdale, and Plaza Companies, as master developer. Plaza Companies and Holualoa Companies are partners on the office buildings. The center is a hub for academic and private entrepreneurship that has revived the previously declining McDowell Corridor neighborhood. Before the center's construction, surrounding companies were relocating and property values decreasing. SkySong itself is on the site of Los Arcos Mall that had been sitting vacant since the mid-1990s.

The center includes five class A four- and six-story office buildings, built between 2008 and 2019, 325 luxury rental apartments, a 157-bed hotel, retail shops, and several restaurants supported by an on-site urban garden. SkySong totals about 1.2 million square feet of commercial office.

The center's sustainable design and extreme heat management features address local climate extremes, demonstrate Arizona State University (ASU)'s renowned built environment programs and initiatives, and are integral to SkySong's ability to attract and retain innovative tenants. "The goal," says Sharon Harper, president, CEO, and cofounder of Plaza Companies, "was to create healthy buildings and healthy environments that would set SkySong apart."

> We started with understanding our climate and understanding the new way that people and companies are spending their days. We are tremendously successful because of that sensitivity.
>
> SHARON HARPER
> President, CEO, and Cofounder, Plaza Companies

Efficient building operations that moderate cooling costs and normalize indoor temperatures are important to SkySong's investors and tenants.

SkySong's development team prioritized heat mitigation and adaptation as part of their tenant attraction and placemaking strategy; the site layout, building design, and shaded pedestrian walkways create a comfortable and creative atmosphere that have helped attract over 57 companies, contributing to a projected regional output of $32 billion.

EXTREME HEAT RESILIENCE STRATEGIES

Organized in four quadrants around an iconic, 150-foot-tall shade structure covering a central plaza, SkySong's buildings are near one another, thus allowing the structures themselves to provide shade to neighboring buildings as well as the pedestrian circulation points around the site. The buildings are oriented to minimize solar heat gain and incorporate multiple facade improvements, including horizontal and vertical shade screens, high-performance window glazing, and small windows on the west and east-facing sides.

Each building capitalizes on the north face with "windows to innovation" where clearer glass components allow additional natural light and views while vertical shade elements prevent glaring sun during parts of the day and year when solar angles reach that face of the building. SkySong buildings 3 and 4 use a standard metal lath in a favorable solar orientation such that the shape of the punch in the panel provides transparency at lower viewing angles and opaqueness at the higher sun angles.

The site layout facilitates efficient pedestrian travel between indoor, air-conditioned lobbies and comfortable and engaging outdoor spaces. Buildings share centralized parking to minimize outside travel time, and pedestrian pathways are well shaded by vegetation, built structures, or both. The centrally located custom 50,000-square-foot shade structure consists of eight conical-shaped pieces covered with tensile fabric supported by eight, 111-foot-long steel legs.[59] Indoor bike parking, showers, and connections to two nearby parks encourage nonmotorized travel.

Developer Sharon Harper also notes that "the efficient operation of the buildings is a key component for investors and tenants and for managing temperature." SkySong has LED lighting as well as daylight harvesting and motion sensors to minimize lighting use. All cooling equipment has nighttime setbacks when buildings are less occupied and staggered start times to minimize peak electric demand. Similarly, SkySong's construction was largely completed early in the morning and partially at night to protect workers' health and ensure daytime heat exposure would not reduce the quality of building materials.

> SkySong is architecturally appealing with functional components for managing heat.
>
> **KOREY WILKES**
> Principal, Butler Design Group

OUTCOME

Achieving the objective of revitalizing the McDowell Corridor neighborhood and spurring innovation, SkySong has generated over $588 million in local economic output with a projected regional output of $32.17 billion by 2046.[60] "The economic output is phenomenal," says Harper. SkySong draws over 5,500 visitors each month and houses 57 companies.

The first two commercial buildings are over 90 percent leased, the more recent SkySong 3 and 4 are 100 percent leased, and the new SkySong 5 is nearly 80 pre-leased. Prominent tenants include multiple enterprising cloud computing firms such as Oracle, photography and imaging equipment supplier Canon, CenturyLink Communications, TicketMaster, Groupon, a research and development subsidiary of Bridgestone Tires, and companies in accelerator programs run by ASU's Office of Entrepreneurship and Innovation. Many of SkySong's early tenants have experienced significant growth and relocated to larger office spaces within the development.

SkySong's buildings are all LEED Silver certified and have achieved Energy Star certification. The heat-conscious landscaping and design creates outdoor amenity spaces that are enjoyed year-round. "Even when it's 115 degrees," says Harper, "there are people sitting in the shade, connected and social."

The "shade sail" that protects SkySong's central plaza was custom-built for the development and is one strategy that ensures outdoor amenity spaces are enjoyable year-round.

OPEN SPACE

FORT WORTH, TEXAS

SUNDANCE SQUARE PLAZA

DEVELOPMENT TEAM:
Sundance Square, Michael Vergason Landscape Architects, DMS Architectural Services

EXTREME HEAT MANAGEMENT FEATURES:
Shade structures, shade trees, water features, reflective materials

YEAR CONSTRUCTED:
2013

SIZE:
2 acres

COST:
$13 million

Sundance Square Plaza is a redeveloped two-acre parking area in downtown Fort Worth where innovative, artistic heat mitigation has directly contributed to the space's tremendous success. The plaza was previously two parking lots (about 195 parking spaces total) separated by Main Street. Opened in November 2013 as part of a long-term, 35-block redevelopment to revitalize Fort Worth, the plaza has become a gathering place, economic driver, and symbol of downtown vibrancy.

The design of the plaza was driven primarily by programming; even when it was parking, events were held there year-round. A key concern was the comfort and experience of the occupants. According to landscape architect Michael Vergason, "Summer heat was part of the discussion from the first conversations."

The goal was to develop an effective, comfortable space that would allow expanded programming but would also be architecturally beautiful.

We thought of it in terms of 'how do we make this a comfortable space for people to gather in before, during, and after their experience downtown?'

JOHNNY CAMPBELL
CEO, Sundance Square

EXTREME HEAT RESILIENCE STRATEGIES

The plaza's most noticeable heat-mitigation feature is its four 86-foot mechanically operable shade umbrellas. Imported from Germany, the umbrellas provide almost 5,800 square feet of shaded space, are illuminated at night by multicolored LED lamps, and can easily be closed on cooler days when the warmth of the sun is welcome. Cedar elm trees provide additional shade along the sidewalks.

SUNDANCE SQUARE

Sundance Square Plaza in downtown Fort Worth is a gathering space that defines the city's character, provides a respite from hot summer temperatures, and accommodates large crowds for parades, festivals, concerts, and fitness classes.

MICHAEL VERGASON ARCHITECTS

Eye-catching, mechanically operated functional shade umbrellas were well worth the extra cost; the plaza's heat-conscious renovation has increased foot traffic, retail sales, and real estate value in the surrounding neighborhood.

MICHAEL VERGASON ARCHITECTS

MICHAEL VERGASON ARCHITECTS

Many of the heat-resilient amenities at Sundance Square Plaza, including the water areas and umbrellas, are adjustable and multipurpose, allowing the park to attract visitors year-round, day and evening.

There are also two water features in the plaza—a large fountain and a water wall—that provide tangible and psychological cooling. Terraces around the park not only are comfortable places to sit but also effectively provide eddies for draining and funneling water toward the vegetation. Red-brick pavers match the nearby roadways and have a higher solar reflective index than the previous black asphalt.

I have never seen a shopping center make such a jump in sales at that age and at that level of maturity. It's been four years of double-digit growth.

JOHNNY CAMPBELL
CEO, Sundance Square

OUTCOME

According to Sundance Square CEO, Johnny Campbell, the plaza was an excellent investment "in terms of driving vibrancy, creating foot traffic and making sales happen." The number of people attending events increased on average by more than 10 times, and retail sales in the vicinity jumped over 20 percent

The plaza has also demonstrably changed people's opinions of and experiences in downtown Fort Worth; it's not uncommon to hear "I'll meet you under the umbrellas." "The city is now seen to have a center," explains Vergason; "it has become a destination."

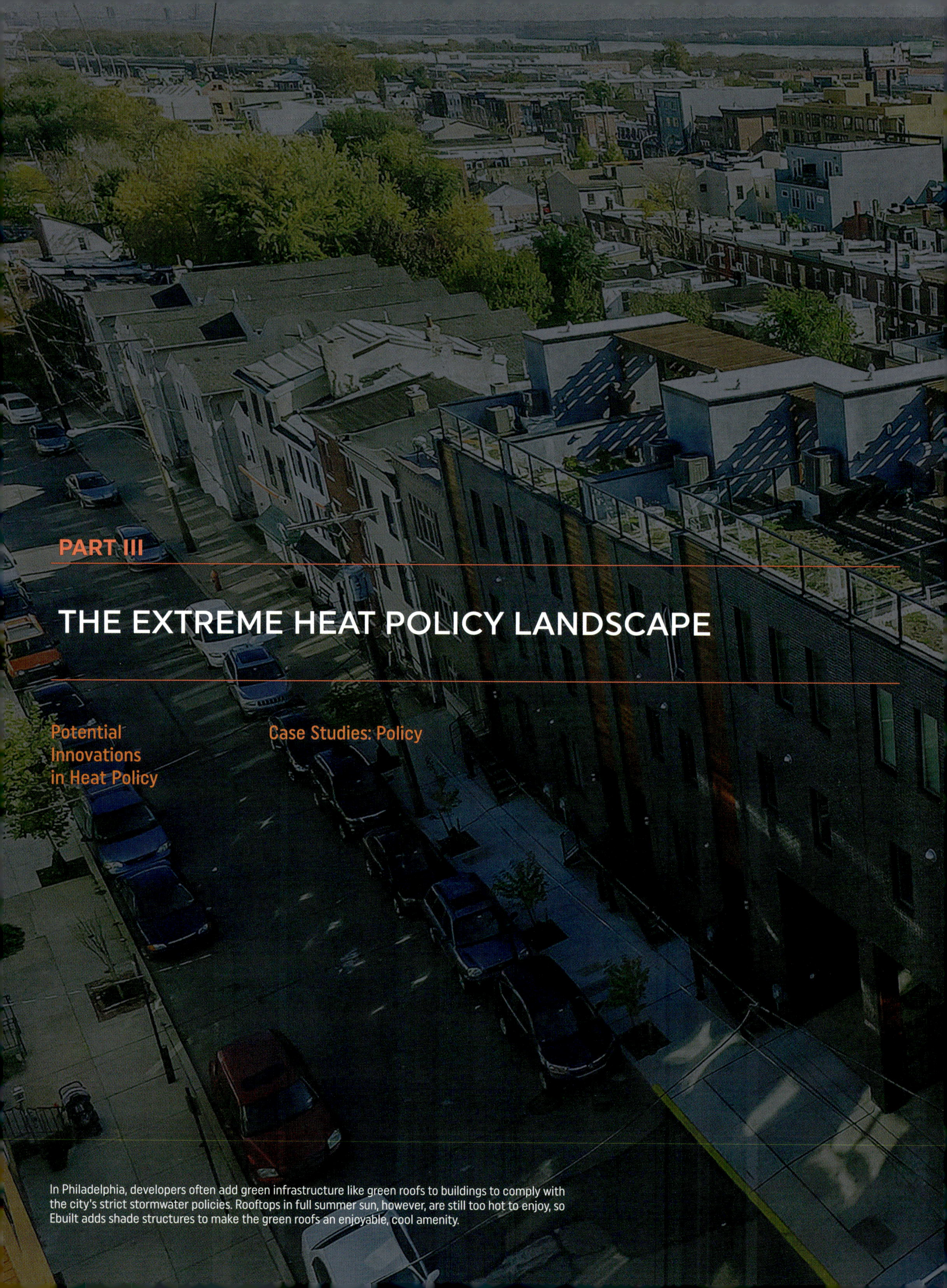

PART III

THE EXTREME HEAT POLICY LANDSCAPE

In Philadelphia, developers often add green infrastructure like green roofs to buildings to comply with the city's strict stormwater policies. Rooftops in full summer sun, however, are still too hot to enjoy, so Ebuilt adds shade structures to make the green roofs an enjoyable, cool amenity.

Public officials increasingly recognize extreme heat as a public health and infrastructure risk and are enacting heat-related policies to safeguard residents and to ensure functioning infrastructure. Although these policies historically addressed social and emergency services, they are gradually addressing issues relevant to land use, real estate, building, and public space design.

Richmond, Virginia, for example, is using new heat vulnerability and heat illness maps to inform a comprehensive update of the city's master plan, including the consideration of zoning for future land uses. Similarly, in May 2019, Miami Beach enacted an ordinance that, among other actions, establishes review criteria to reduce the heat island effect of buildings and waives certain application fees for developments that use sustainable construction materials and vegetation that reduces UHIE. As developers, owners, and investors invest in site-level heat resilience, tracking and responding to regional-level investments may complement and enhance the value of their efforts.

Many cities with existing requirements related to extreme heat mitigation are updating them to higher, stricter standards. Requirements or incentives for cool roofs and shade cover are two common real estate–related heat-mitigation policies that have recently been updated in multiple locations, including in Los Angeles and Phoenix. Increasingly, historically temperate locations such as Chicago (cool roof requirements) and Portland, Oregon (green roof requirements) are adding heat-related policies.[1]

Motivation for Policy Change

Public officials concerned about heat often cite triggering events such as heat waves with high mortality, an increasing number of high-heat days, and better data quantifying these local climate changes as motivation for policy action.[2] "We knew that heat was a problem," says Kate Johnson, chief of D.C.'s Green Buildings and Climate division, "but the climate projections confirmed our worst fears in terms of how the problem could get worse."

In San Francisco, for example, where UHIE contributed to a 78°F temperature differential across the city during a 2017 September heat wave, the "big focus is the residential piece—the homes and apartment complexes with southern-facing frontages that do not have air conditioning and especially are in areas of the city with intense heat island effects," says Daniel Homsey, director of neighborhood resilience for the City and County of San Francisco, "San Francisco has traditionally had a cooler climate, but as we shift to becoming a warmer city, a lot of development decisions that were made in the '30s, '40s, '50s, and '60s in cooler conditions now manifest into real barriers to us protecting the health and well-being of residents."

Public officials also cite Moody's consideration of climate preparedness in bond ratings as a reason for mitigation and adaptation programs and projects.[3] Demonstrating how a city is addressing extreme weather "ensures that our bond rating is going to stay lower," explains Marie Light, program manager for the Pima County (Arizona) Department of Environmental Quality. Since Moody's announcement in 2017, 17 percent of city mitigation projects address heat, drought, or storms (compared with 60 percent of cities that report projects managing flood risks).[4]

> The big solution is in the urban environments.
>
> CHRIS CALOTT
> Developer/Architect, Infill Solutions/Calott + Gilfford Architecture

RESEARCH IN FOCUS: THE BUSINESS CASE FOR CITIES

The benefits of implementing multiple heat island mitigation strategies in El Paso, Philadelphia, and Washington, D.C., far exceed the costs; a 2018 study led by Greg Kats, current president of consulting and green investment firm Capital E who earlier helped create LEED, estimated that the net present value (NPV) of widespread implementation of cool roofs, green roofs, solar photovoltaic arrays, reflective pavements, and urban canopy could total in the billions.[5]

Specifically, the calculated NPV "of citywide adoption of these technologies ranges from $538 million for El Paso to $1.8 billion for Washington, D.C., and $3.6 billion for Philadelphia." If an estimated avoided loss for tourism is included (an area of uncertainty, so losses are estimated), the expected NPV for D.C. rises to $4.9 billion and for Philadelphia to $8.4 billion. The findings acknowledge that payback time and the net benefit per square foot for each strategy vary greatly.

Researchers calculated the costs (installation, maintenance) and benefits (energy savings, heat-related mortality reduction, employment, and others) for each smart surface technology then aggregated them on a citywide scale. The calculations do not take into account several unquantified factors such as the "downwind cooling effect," that is, the regional benefits that would occur if multiple cities implemented smart surfaces.

Value of Implementing Smart Surfaces Technology in Three Cities

CATEGORY	PRESENT VALUE OVER 40-YEAR ANALYSIS PERIOD (2015)		
	WASHINGTON, D.C.	PHILADELPHIA	EL PASO
Costs	$838 million	$2.38 billion	$1.62 billion
Benefits	$2.65 billion	$5.96 billion	$2.16 billion
Net present value	$1.81 billion	$3.58 billion	$538 million

POTENTIAL INNOVATIONS IN HEAT POLICY

Potential heat-mitigation policies relevant to the real estate sector include the following:

CITYWIDE TEMPERATURE REDUCTION GOALS: Similar to GHG emissions goals, several cities across the world have set temperature reduction targets. Los Angeles's goal is to reduce UHI by 1.7°F by 2025 and average temperature 3°F by 2035.[6] Melbourne, Australia's target is to reduce the city's average temperature 7°F by 2030.[7] To achieve its goal, Los Angeles has begun by focusing on increasing tree cover and incentivizing residential upgrades. In 2018, for example, Los Angeles announced a $100 million residential insulation rebate program.[8]

EXPANDED URBAN CANOPY AND GREENING PROGRAMS: Numerous cities have implemented tree canopy programs, including impactful and high-profile public greening projects in New Orleans, Charlotte, Houston, Baltimore, New York City, Chicago, and Los Angeles. Some cities with aggressive tree canopy and greening policies have, for the most part, maxed out public land, so future policy may target privately held land. The Philadelphia Water Department, for example, is currently working with developers to green privately owned curb cuts.[9] Other additional focus areas include using climate projections and heat vulnerability maps to direct greening resources to areas that need it most.

COOL WALL STANDARDS: The state of California, the U.S. Green Building Council via LEED (Leadership in Energy and Environmental Design), the Environmental Protection Agency via Energy Star, the American Society of Heating and Air-Conditioning Engineers (ASHRAE), and the Cool Roof Rating Council are considering new or enhanced cool wall provisions. Similar to reflective standards for cool roofs, these entities may rate or govern the reflectance of wall products.[10]

In New York, 50 percent of the urban forest is on private land. In Los Angeles, it's more like 90 percent. We need to engage with the private sector to incentivize canopy growth and mitigate heat effects.

CONNIE CHUNG
Principal, HR&A

VALERIE QUEEN-BLAZITZ, PEXELS

Through policies and incentives, cities can create opportunities for developers to implement heat-conscious design elements like green walls.

REBATES AND INCENTIVE PROGRAMS: Some cities are considering increasing the value of available rebates to encourage more widespread adoption of heat-mitigation strategies, such as green roofs, by the private sector.[11]

THERMAL COMFORT POLICIES: Cities are beginning to consider how to maintain or increase thermal comfort in the residential sector. These are largely exploratory processes; Cincinnati, for example, committed to evaluating new requirements for residential air conditioning in its 2018 sustainability plan. In *OneNYC*, New York City assessed the feasibility of establishing "a citywide maximum allowable indoor temperature in residential facilities and supportive housing for vulnerable populations."[12] And Washington's 2019 *Resilient DC* plan establishes the objective that "all new buildings [are] to be built climate ready by 2032" in part by "strengthen[ing] requirements that would address increased heat and flood risk (such as passive survivability or a building's ability to support its occupants in the event of a power outage)."[13]

OCCUPATIONAL HAZARD POLICIES: Although "there are currently no specific OSHA [Occupational Safety and Health Administration] standards for occupational heat exposure," there are a number of related safety requirements for employees exposed to high temperatures.[14] The first indoor heat safety law took effect January 2017 in California and applies to workplaces with ambient air temperatures above 90°F or workers who are performing moderately heavy labor at 80°F or above.[15] Other organizations, such as ASHRAE, also provide thermal comfort standards.

> **Heat-mitigation measures are often hybridized projects that align with stormwater management, air quality control, and energy efficiency.**
>
> JILLIAN KIRN
> Shareholder, Greenberg Traurig LLP

MITIGATING SOCIAL ISOLATION: SOCIAL SERVICES AND COMMUNITY BUILDING

Social isolation is a major risk factor in heat-related mortality, so governments and nonprofits are implementing programs and policies that encourage community familiarity and neighborhood cohesion.

One event that increases emergency preparedness and helps neighbors build stronger relationships with each other is San Francisco's Neighborfest: The World's Greatest Block Party. Founded in 2015 by multiple local nonprofits partnering with several city agencies, Neighborfest has more than 35 participating communities that engage in activities to build social capital, train residents to become efficient conveners, and develop an asset registry for critical neighborhood resources. Residents even organize the event using the roles of the "Incident Command System," the best practice chain of command for first responders worldwide.[16]

This approach is also related to new thinking about the role of cooling centers. Although strategically locating and building cooling centers in areas of high heat vulnerability remains a key response strategy, cities have observed that many heat-vulnerable populations (especially seniors) have difficulty traveling to cooling centers, are reluctant to travel to new places during times of stress, and are often exposed to additional heat during that commute.

Many cities are now considering how they can alter already frequented public spaces to serve as "resilience hubs" and places of respite. "We need to think about what else can we do to make community facilities places where people can shelter in place on hot days," explains Kizzy Charles-Guzman, deputy director, NYC Mayor's Office of Resiliency.

SAN FRANCISCO DEPARTMENT OF NEIGHBORHOOD RESILIENCE

Participants in San Francisco's Neighborfest work together to map assets available locally in their community that they can use or share during events such as heat waves or power outages to stay healthy and safe.

CHICAGO AFTER THE HEAT WAVE

The Chicago Heat Wave of July 1995 remains the deadliest heat wave in modern U.S. history. From Thursday, July 13 to Monday, July 16, daytime temperatures hovered between the high 90s and low triple digits, hitting a maximum 106°F on July 13 with a humidity-driven heat index of 125°F.[17] It was so hot that the fire department was called in to hose down dehydrated children riding in school buses while city workers watered bridges to prevent them from locking when plates expanded.

The health system became overwhelmed; every paramedic and ambulance was in service, and 23 emergency rooms stopped accepting new patients. Energy use skyrocketed; multiple transformers blew, leaving 49,000 without power or air conditioning. Residents opened 3,000 hydrants to cool off, leading to the loss of water pressure as well as electricity in some areas.[18]

The heat killed 739 in the city that week; a disproportionate number were elderly, low-income, and/or African American residents of inner-city neighborhoods that had suffered disinvestment and community fragmentation over decades.[19] Substandard housing, lack of air conditioning, lack of transportation access, preexisting illness, fear of crime and violence, and social isolation were common risk factors.

Chicago responded by consolidating its emergency response structure to more quickly recognize threats and mobilize resources as well as implementing a procedure of door-to-door checks on elderly residents, providing free bus transportation to cooling centers, and establishing a heat advisory system. Chicago also enacted UHI mitigation policies such as green roof grants, a green and porous paving alleyway program, and landscape ordinances mandating tree planting on parkways, parking lots, and loading docks.

SHUTTERSTOCK

After a devastating heat wave in 1995, Chicago improved its ability to respond to extreme heat events and took steps to mitigate the urban heat island effect through urban greening policy.

COMMUNITY ENGAGEMENT AND CONNECTION PROGRAMS: Building on a growing body of research demonstrating the importance of social cohesion to disaster resilience, select cities (and designers) are prioritizing programs and patterns of urban development that enhance community. For example, San Francisco is an organizing partner in a block party–style program called Neighborfest that introduces residents to each other and simultaneously teaches disaster response skills. Likewise, Washington, D.C., is considering launching a Resilience Corps that would deploy paid neighborhood captains to organize neighborhood-based services and events as well as promote existing programs that lower climate-related risks for at-risk populations.[20]

Most city governments are not acting alone to reduce excess heat. Neighboring jurisdictions, utilities, developers, contractors, and local building owners are collaborating to create incentives for communities to reduce urban heat and mainstream these practices.[21] For example, the Sacramento Municipal Utility District (SMUD) operated the United States' first cool roof program for commercial buildings from 2001 through 2005 and continues a free tree installation program for low-income customers that has planted over a half-million trees in the Sacramento area since 1990.[22]

> **Heat casualties tend to be invisible without data.**
>
> LARRY FALKIN
> Director, Cincinnati's Office of Environment and Sustainability

ZONING FOR HEAT MITIGATION: GOWANUS TECHNICAL ASSISTANCE PANEL

Supported by the New York Community Trust, in 2017 ULI New York partnered with the Fifth Avenue Committee, a South Brooklyn community-based organization, to identify urban heat island reduction land use actions and design standards as part of an expected rezoning in Gowanus. Previously an industrial area, Gowanus is a Brooklyn neighborhood with a high heat vulnerability index, a high proportion of poor and underserved residents, and a history of environmental contamination. The rezoning is expected to increase the neighborhood's density and presents opportunities to incorporate "heat resilience" best practices in new development.

"There's no better time than now to focus on environmental justice needs and the health and overall quality of life for residents," wrote Michelle de la Uz, executive director of the Fifth Avenue Committee, in an op-ed following the technical assistance panel.[23]

The technical assistance panel recommended a number of UHI mitigation strategies and targets, including the following:

- Achieve 20 percent tree canopy cover.
- Convert a large parking lot to a park with green space, shade trees, swimming pool and/or water play area, and a tree nursery to propagate trees through the neighborhood.
- Reconfigure the main transportation corridor to improve pedestrian safety, add shaded green space, and reduce transportation-related waste heat.
- Establish zoning policies that require the sorts of building massing and form that allow ventilation and airflow through the community and introduce incentives such as increased floor/area ratio for incorporation of heat-mitigation techniques.

SOFIA GUERRERO/ULI NY

To provide input on proposed rezoning, ULI members in partnership with New York Institute of Technology's Urban Climate Lab evaluate likely future development scenarios to help calculate the benefits of implementing best practice neighborhood strategies for mitigation and adaptation.

CASE STUDIES: POLICY

ULI/JACKIE CANALES

In addition to providing public amenities and acting as an important commercial corridor, the San Antonio River Walk helps mitigate the urban heat island effect and reduce the impact of extreme heat. In historically hot cities like San Antonio, public parks provide much-needed sanctuary with shade, green space, and other amenities.

POLICY

NEW YORK, NEW YORK

COOL NEIGHBORHOODS

YEAR IMPLEMENTED:
2017

Cool Neighborhoods NYC is a strategy developed by the Mayor's Office of Resiliency to provide and target additional funding and to coordinate multiple extreme heat mitigation and adaptation projects. The objective of Cool Neighborhoods NYC is to "help keep New Yorkers safe during hot weather, mitigate urban heat island effect drivers and protect against the worst impacts of rising temperatures from climate change."

Although in a temperate climate zone, New York City's average temperature is expected to increase by almost 6°F by 2050, and there are already 450 heat-related emergency department visits, 150 heat-related hospital admissions, and 13 heatstroke deaths in the city on average each year. On top of this background temperature increase from climate change, the urban heat island effect makes New York City about 3°F warmer than its less urban surroundings.[24]

> Rising temperatures continue to threaten the health of all New Yorkers, but particularly older adults, those without access to air conditioning, and those with a variety of health conditions.
>
> BILL DE BLASIO
> Mayor, New York City
> Cool Neighborhoods NYC

The additional degrees are a significant concern for the 10 percent of New Yorkers without home air conditioning and for residents in public housing where only half of households self-report having AC.[25] However, this number may be artificially low because, per HUD regulations, the New York City Housing Authority (NYCHA) charges a monthly fee for each voluntarily reported AC unit. NYCHA's development-specific AC counts have historically found an average of 1.5 AC units per apartment. Because 95 percent of NYCHA households do not pay their own electric bills, cost of electricity is likely not a determining factor in AC adoption.

Despite the complexities of quantifying AC use in public housing, the strategies established by Cool Neighborhoods NYC target the city's communities that are most vulnerable to heat. The NYC Mayor's Office of Resiliency uses the results of an intensive heat vulnerability mapping collaboration between the NYC Department of Health and Mental Hygiene and Columbia University to direct cool design interventions and tailor heat resilience social programs.

Cool Neighborhoods NYC uses interagency data to deliver extreme heat mitigation strategies, including tree planting, cool roofs, and social services, to the neighborhoods with the most need.

NYC MAYOR'S OFFICE OF RESILIENCE

Cool Neighborhoods NYC employs local job seekers to install cool roofs, so the program provides residents with employment and job training as well as helps decrease indoor air temperatures and the need for air conditioning.

EXTREME HEAT RESILIENCE STRATEGIES

Cool Neighborhoods NYC establishes temperature mitigation and adaptation strategies in three areas: the built environment; public education and outreach; and data collection and monitoring. Beyond the 2007 Million TreesNYC initiative, NYC is dedicating over $100 million through Cool Neighborhoods NYC for targeted tree planting along streets, in parks, and in forests through 2021. Many of the trees will be planted in the South Bronx, Northern Manhattan, and Central Brooklyn neighborhoods, which have comparatively little vegetation coverage and the highest levels of heat vulnerability.

> **We are bringing health and climate data into urban planning and policymaking to achieve environmental equity goals.**
>
> KIZZY CHARLES-GUZMAN
> Deputy Director
> Mayor's Office of Resiliency

NYC is also targeting its cool roof programs to heat-vulnerable neighborhoods, leveraging its green infrastructure programs, improving cooling center signage, enacting policy to require green roofs in buildings, and monitoring summer temperatures in several communities with high heat vulnerability to understand variability at the neighborhood level.

In an effort to reach homebound residents, those with preexisting medical conditions, and seniors who are typically at higher risk during extreme heat events, NYC is partnering with home care agencies and community health organizations to train attendants on how to recognize and treat heat stress. NYC has also formed partnerships with three community organizations, funding them to implement a pilot Be a Buddy initiative in which participants are trained to assist at-risk adults, to identify potentially isolated New Yorkers, and to proactively communicate heat-related health messages and warnings.

OUTCOME

As of April 2019, NYC has installed more than 10 million square feet of reflective, cool roofs. The city estimates that cool roofs can lower building AC costs by 10 to 30 percent and reduce indoor air temperatures by up to 30 percent during the summer.[26] In addition, NYC hires 70 local job seekers per year to install the reflective rooftop coatings and provides the employees with training and the opportunity to obtain industry-relevant certifications. The new Be a Buddy pilot to assist at-risk adults also launched in 2018 and street tree plantings in many heat-vulnerable NYC neighborhoods are ongoing.

Interagency coordination is key to the establishment and implementation of Cool Neighborhoods NYC. "What's innovative about our work," says Mayor's Office of Resiliency deputy director Kizzy Charles-Guzman, "is that we took data that already existed in various agencies and brought it together in a way that hadn't been done before in our sustainability planning.

Charles-Guzman's recommendation to other cities that want to address temperature risks: mayoral offices must gather and analyze agency data and commit to developing and implementing an integrative, community-specific approach.

TORONTO, CANADA

GREEN ROOF BYLAW AND ECO-ROOF INCENTIVE

YEAR IMPLEMENTED:
2009

Toronto was the first city in North America to require and govern the construction of green roofs on new development. The Green Roof Bylaw (which includes a Green Roof Construction Standard) and the parallel Eco-Roof Incentive Program are responsible for more than 1.2 million square feet of new green space, an estimated reduction in citywide temperature, and widespread promotion of cool roofs.

"We have cold winters, but we also have very hot summers, and given that we're in an intense urban environment, temperatures are exacerbated by the urban heat island effect," explains Shayna Stott, an environmental planner with the city's Planning Division.

In 2005, Toronto commissioned Ryerson University to study the impact of greening all of Toronto's available large rooftop space. The results revealed an estimated potential urban heat island reduction of 0.5–2°C (about 1–9°F).

Toronto began encouraging green roofs on city and privately owned properties through public education, financial incentives, and the development approval process in 2006. In 2009, Toronto adopted the municipal bylaw, which took effect in 2010 for most building types and in 2012 for new industrial development.

After passing the Green Roof Bylaw, Toronto installed the city's largest publicly accessible green roof atop City Hall.

EXTREME HEAT RESILIENCE STRATEGIES

The city of Toronto hosted numerous engagement sessions that included both industry and community stakeholders when developing the bylaw and associated Toronto Green Roof Construction Standard.

The bylaw established a graduated green roof requirement, ranging from 20 to 60 percent coverage, depending on building size, for all commercial, institutional, and residential buildings with a minimum gross floor area of 2,000 square meters. Consideration of the local planning context resulted in exemptions for residential developments under six stories tall and an option for industrial building owners that allows them to choose between a 10 percent green roof or a 100 percent cool roof with other stormwater retention measures sufficient to capture 50 percent of annual rainfall.

The bylaw's construction standard established minimum requirements for numerous factors and mandatory provisions in 14 categories, including green roof assembly, waterproofing and drainage, vegetation selection and performance, and occupant health and safety.

For building owners who cannot or choose not to meet the green roof requirements, the Green Roof Bylaw offers a cash in lieu alternative. Toronto uses these payments to directly fund the Eco-Roof Incentive Program.

The Eco-Roof Incentive Program promotes green and cool roofs by providing funds to retrofit roofs on existing buildings. The incentive program is open to school and nonprofit buildings as well as buildings smaller than 2,000 square meters. To be eligible, green roofs must meet the Green Roof Construction Standard, and cool roofing material for low slope roofs must have at least a solar reflectance index (SRI) rating of 78 and for high-slope roofs an SRI of 25 or greater.

The incentive program's success is owed in part to its dedicated funding stream and substantial grants; eligible green roof projects can receive $100 per square meter up to $100,000, and cool roof projects can receive $2 to $5 per square meter up to $50,000.

OUTCOME

By replacing dark, impervious roof surfaces with soil and vegetation, a green roof will lower ambient temperatures, reduce interior temperature fluctuation, improve air quality, reduce building energy use, retain stormwater, and create attractive and useful outdoor amenities. Critically, by reducing extreme temperature fluctuations, green roofs also extend the life of a roof from the traditional about 20 years to about 40 years.

The impact in Toronto is significant. About 620 new green roof permits have been required under the bylaw, totaling over 5.4 million square feet of new green roof area. The incentive program has provided funding for more than 70 green roofs and 336 cool roofs since 2010.

The greening of just 5 percent of the city's area via green and cool roofs is estimated to lower citywide temperature by about 1°F with a greater temperature reduction in high-density areas and with a direct 4–5°C roof surface cooling effect. Each year, the green roofs also save over 1.5 million kilowatt-hours in energy for building owners, reduce 435,000 cubic feet of stormwater runoff, and avoid 220 metric tons of GHG emissions.[27]

We attribute that success to the early industry consultation that occurred, leadership within the development industry to build capacity, and development of a requirement that was tailored to work well within the local existing regulatory structures that development faces.

SHAYNA STOTT
Environmental Planner,
City of Toronto

Since implementation, Toronto has made only minor policy adjustments to the regulation and the incentive program. For example, after learning that the cost of the structural assessments was a barrier for smaller developments, Toronto implemented an additional structural assessment grant.

"The major lesson learned," for Toronto says Stott, "is that implementation has gone fairly smoothly."

FLICKR, PADRAIC

Green roofs deliver benefits at the building and city levels by reducing temperatures, managing stormwater, mitigating greenhouse gas emissions, and decreasing energy demand.

LOS ANGELES, CALIFORNIA

COOL SURFACES: ROOFS AND ROADS

YEAR IMPLEMENTED:
2014

Los Angeles is the first U.S. city to set a citywide temperature reduction goal, and switching to cool surfaces is a key strategy for achieving that goal. Los Angeles's goal is to reduce the urban heat island effect by 1.7°F by 2025 and average temperature 3°F by 2035, but the city is 40 percent covered by pavement.[28] Los Angeles's reflective paving program, which targets both rooftops and public streets, complements other UHI reduction programs including a Million Trees initiative and integrated planning with the Department of Health.

"The lived experience of Los Angeles is that the place is getting hotter," explains Greg Spotts, assistant director of the Los Angeles Bureau of Street Services (StreetsLA). "When we got started, I thought that the main potential of cool surfaces was reduced indoor temperatures, reduced air conditioning use, and reduced carbon emissions."

> An epidemiologist showed us the trends in heat-related illnesses and deaths and how those trends are supposed to go through the roof as cities get hotter. That created a very powerful drive.
>
> GREG SPOTTS
> Assistant Director, Los Angeles Bureau of Street Services

EXTREME HEAT RESILIENCE STRATEGIES

The Los Angeles Green Building Code's cool roof requirement was implemented in 2014 for residential buildings. Managed by the city's Department of Buildings and Safety, residential buildings must meet minimum values for 30-year aged solar reflectance and thermal emittance, a combination of two numbers measuring both how much light energy a material bounces back, or solar reflectance, and how well a material rejects heat, or thermal emittance.[29]

The original SRI standard at the county level about doubled the reflectance of a traditional asphalt shingle and set different rates for flat and steep roofs. In 2018, the city of Los Angeles independently increased the SRI requirements to 0.25 for steep slope and 0.8 for flat roofs.

In addition, the Los Angeles Department of Water and Power (LADWP), a city-owned utility, offers cool roof rebates between $0.20 and $0.30 per square foot to eligible single- and multifamily residential customers.

In a city dominated by roads, light-colored, cool pavement may help Los Angeles achieve its ambitious temperature reduction goals.

Pilot tests in Los Angeles demonstrate both benefits and challenges of cool pavement. The city is continuing to evaluate, refine, and expand this heat-mitigation technique.

Partnering with a California-based manufacturer of a gray, highly reflective coating, StreetsLA began a three-part test to confirm that the reflective topcoat would adhere to road safety standards. Following rigorous testing in the StreetsLA Materials Testing Lab and a pilot on a parking lot, StreetsLA secured $150,000 in funding in early 2017 to coat one residential city block in each of the 15 city districts.

OUTCOME

The cool roof requirements have resulted in a minimum of 20,000 new cool roofs in Los Angeles. "The feedback we're getting is universally positive," says Jonathan Parfrey, executive director of Climate Resolve, a nonprofit organization that helped define the new benchmarks. "No one is saying they have to pay more for a cool roof because the properties are getting an immediate payback and paying less on utility bills." Los Angeles's building code has also changed the materials market regionally; manufacturers have virtually stopped supplying roofing materials that do not meet the city's SRI standards.

> **The properties are getting an immediate payback and paying less on utility bills.**
>
> JONATHAN PARFREY
> Executive Director, Climate Resolve

At the street level, the cool paving has decreased surface temperatures by about 10°F although the tests have revealed other challenges. Half the city block pilot projects, for example, were recoated by the topcoat manufacturer with a slightly altered reflective formula in 2018 to address observed sealant flaking and decreased reflectance in some of the test sites. The StreetsLA Materials Testing Lab continues to visit each site once a month to take temperature measurements.

StreetsLA has enjoyed significant press and social media attention around the world. The first installation of cool paint on a city block coincided with the hottest weekend of that year to date; StreetsLA did five impromptu interviews with local TV stations that day. Since then, the pavement testing has been featured in the national and international press as well as in a short ATTN video that drew over 20 million views on Facebook (compared to StreetsLA's typical 5,000 to 10,000 views).

The next two phases of testing began in early summer 2019. In May, StreetsLA began testing cool streets at neighborhood level, coating about nine adjacent city blocks in three different residential areas.

StreetsLA is also planning to evaluate reflective paving as one solution in a community-driven one-mile cooling initiative around a bus rapid transit station in California's San Fernando Valley.[30] The initiative is funded by a $354,000 Adaptation Planning Grant from the California Department of Transportation and a minimum in-kind $46,000 match from the city.[31] The transit station serves a population that may be at risk from extreme heat; the neighborhood is a local "hot spot," and residents are predominantly cost-burdened renters, highly dependent on public transit and active transportation, Hispanic, and have a median income of about 60 percent of California's median household income. The results of this "last mile" cooling project will inform Los Angeles's planned future work to update the climate adaptation and land use components of 35 community plans.

CINCINNATI, OHIO

URBAN CANOPY POLICY

YEAR IMPLEMENTED:
1981

Cincinnati created a dedicated funding stream for its urban forestry program in 1981 that has enabled the city to maintain a high percentage of its tree canopy. Heat mitigation is a key reason tree canopy is a priority. Although Cincinnati has a temperate climate and harsh, cold winters, the urban heat island effect can make the city up to 17°F hotter than nearby rural areas during the summer.[32]

According to Larry Falkin, the director of Cincinnati's Office of Environment and Sustainability, tree canopy is "the most straightforward strategy" for reducing the urban heat island effect." Cincinnati's 2018 Green Cincinnati Plan states that urban canopy cover "will help minimize the effects of urban heat islands," "reduce the cost of cooling for residents," and "reduce the concentrations of air pollutants," as well as help mitigate flood, stormwater, and landslide risks.

In addition to mitigating climate and environmental hazards, Cincinnati prioritizes maintaining a healthy urban tree canopy as a public safety and social equity strategy. "It's very important to make sure that the stormwater, heat island effect mitigation, simple habitat and air quality benefits of trees are shared equally among the population," says Crystal Courtney, Cincinnati's urban forestry supervisor in the Parks Department.

Cincinnati maintains its tree canopy cover and mitigates the urban heat island effect through a dedicated annual assessment based on property frontage along the public right-of-way.

EXTREME HEAT RESILIENCE STRATEGIES

Cincinnati uses an assessment that allows it to collect an annual levy for the control, planting, care, and maintenance of shade trees. This regulation is unique to Ohio and is guided at the state level by Revised Code 727. The Urban Forestry Assessment began with the inception of the Urban Forestry Division in 1981, requiring property owners to pay $0.05 per linear foot of frontage along a public right-of-way. The assessment follows the same process today and applies equally to every sector, including private, public, nonprofit, and government-owned land.

In 2018, the City Council voted to increase the requirement to $0.21 per foot. In total, the assessment amount has gradually increased 32 percent over almost 40 years. The increase covers the inflation costs of maintenance, additional tree plantings to address canopy loss caused by the tree-killing Emerald Ash Borer beetle, and achieving Cincinnati's increased urban canopy cover goals. In its 2018 sustainability plan, Cincinnati established a goal to increase the citywide tree canopy coverage to at least 40 percent and to ensure that canopy cover is at least 30 percent in all residential neighborhoods.

The assessment process is governed by three city ordinances, which are renewed annually. The Board of Park Commissioners and the City Council approve the annual assessment level.

Owners see the charge as an individual item on their property assessment. "The typical situation is a 50-foot property frontage times 21 cents plus a county admin fee," says Urban Forestry Specialist Robin Hunt. "There are some cases where property owners have up to three sides with the right-of-way; however, the average homeowner pays $15 each year." Property owners are notified if they owe $250 or more, but there is no maximum payment amount.[33]

Cincinnati has one of the most successful urban forestry programs in the country, which is helping the city achieve its goal of 40 percent citywide tree cover.

Urban trees provide essential environmental services by minimizing the urban heat island effect, reducing air pollution, and managing stormwater. Cincinnati's dedicated funding stream for urban forestry enables the city to grow and maintain these critical assets.

> Cincinnati has a big advantage because in our Parks Department, we have an Urban Forestry Division and we have a dedicated funding stream for our urban forest.
>
> **LARRY FALKIN**
> Director, Cincinnati's Office of Environment and Sustainability

OUTCOME

The outcome of the well-funded program is a higher than national average urban canopy cover; with 38 percent tree cover as of 2010, Cincinnati is close to meeting its goal of 40 percent citywide tree cover.

The assessment levy funds the Urban Forestry section of Cincinnati's Parks Department (including all staff) and makes possible regular tree maintenance and analysis of progress. The funds give "the opportunity to focus on what we want our urban forests to look like," elaborates Courtney. "It allows us to work as experts in urban forestry and manage contracts as they relate to tree maintenance and the continuation of the next generation of forest."

The Urban Forestry Division inspects and maintains about 12,000 trees each year. Even with preventive maintenance, Urban Forestry uses funds from the property assessment to respond to about 800 emergency calls each year following extreme rainfall or other storm events to, for example, clear tree-blocked roadways. "Preparedness for emergency tree maintenance is something that needs to be continually done for public safety," says Hunt.

The assessment also enables the completion of an Urban Tree Canopy Assessment every 10 years that combines GIS canopy distribution data with census data. Cincinnati uses the results to guide management decisions and to allocate new trees in the neighborhoods with lower canopy cover. Beginning in 2020, the Urban Forestry Program will partner with the Ohio Division of Natural Resources to include fine particulate matter (a known cause of increased asthma rates) and urban heat island

Parks and open spaces provide cool and comfortable areas of respite that help ensure that cities remain livable and enjoyable even on high-temperature days.

CONCLUSION: BUILDING FOR A WARMER FUTURE

In the first month of 2019, the year this report was printed, 33 hottest temperature records were broken around the world while no coldest temperature records were surpassed.[1] Many communities are likely to experience the trend toward higher temperature days; longer, more frequent heat waves; and intensified impacts in cities because of the projected effects of climate change and continued urban development.

The built environment greatly influences people's experience as they visit, work, play, and live—especially in urban areas. With thoughtful design and consideration of temperature-related risks, real estate and land use practitioners can mitigate the effects of extreme heat on people and infrastructure, realize the business benefits of early resilience leadership, and contribute to the long-term success and livability of communities.

ACTIONABLE NEXT STEPS

There is no "silver bullet" or "one size fits all" strategy for achieving heat resilience, but developers, owners, property managers, and policymakers across the United States can take the following steps.

- Assess and monitor long-term risks from extreme heat over the lifetime of a building, development, or city to understand the likely impacts on users and community members.
- Implement heat-resilient development strategies and policies such as the following:
  - Strategically maximize shade—through built or natural cover—for all buildings and public spaces.
  - Tactically encourage airflow for optimum ventilation inside and around a building or development.
  - Prioritize the preservation of green space on new development parcels.
  - Create green space on new and existing development parcels if appropriate for local climate conditions and water availability.
  - Install green or light-colored roofing.
  - Consider design strategies, such as operable windows or cooling systems connected to backup power sources, that help maintain safe indoor temperatures during hot-weather power outages.
  - Evaluate the need for air conditioning and, if warranted, install the most environmentally-friendly option available to minimize GHG emissions.
  - Use energy-efficient equipment and principles to minimize heat gain, reduce energy use, and manage waste heat.

- Contribute to community preparedness and response strategies for extreme heat:
  - Organize or otherwise support events that contribute to company and/or community "neighborliness" so that users have a social network and are aware of resources before an emergency occurs.
  - Develop, test, and regularly update emergency response and business continuity plans.
- Track the impact of extreme heat mitigation and adaptation strategies and share lessons learned.

The real estate and land use sectors have the potential to alleviate many of the negative consequences of extreme heat and develop heat-resilient buildings, open spaces, infrastructure, and cities that keep residents cool and safe. Implementing mitigation strategies that reduce temperatures and adaptation strategies that increase coping ability may also help "future-proof" real estate in vulnerable markets; lower operations and management costs; improve tenant and occupant experience; and otherwise differentiate real estate projects.

Increasing urban tree cover provides natural shading, reduces the impact of extreme heat, and makes for more attractive city streetscapes.

There are many resilience strategies, such as these window shades and light-colored walls at Edison Eastlake in Arizona, that contribute to occupant well-being, reduce operating costs, and may future-proof developments against the negative consequences of extreme heat.

Public parks like Tulsa's Gathering Place provide more than a fun space to play, socialize, and relax. They also enhance neighborhoods by making them more resilient to extreme heat and other impacts of climate change.

ACKNOWLEDGMENTS

Many individuals, companies, and organizations in ULI's membership and beyond contributed to this report by participating in interviews, providing images, or otherwise supplying information and sharing their perspectives. This report would not have been possible without the generous support of The JPB Foundation.

ULI greatly appreciates the participation of experts from the following organizations in the creation of this report:

AECOM

Arizona State University

ARUP

Austin Commercial

Autocase

Butler Design Group

Calott + Gifford Architecture

Capital E

City and County of San Francisco

City of Cincinnati Sustainability Department

City of Cincinnati Urban Forestry Department

City of Phoenix Housing Department

City of Richmond, Virginia

Climate Resolve

Crystal City BID

D.C. Department of Energy & Environment

Design Workshop

Ebuilt

Elementa Engineering

Fifth Avenue Committee

FourTwentySeven

Gensler

Georgia Institute of Technology

GLHN Architects & Engineers

Global Cool Cities Alliance

Goldenberg Group

Gowanus Neighborhood Coalition for Justice

Greenberg Traurig

Harvard University Graduate School of Design

Heat Island Group at Lawrence Berkeley National Laboratory

Hilton Anatole Hotel

Hoare Lee

Houston Midtown Redevelopment Authority

HR&A

Infill Solutions

Integral Group

JBG Smith

Jupiter Intelligence

LandSec

Los Angeles Bureau of Street Services

Michael Vergason Landscape Architects

Mithun Inc.

Neighborhood of Affordable Housing

New York Institute of Technology

NYC Mayor's Office of Resiliency

Oficinaa

Onion Flats LLC

Pima County Department of Environmental Quality

Pima County Regional Flood Control District

Plaza Companies

Sacramento Municipal Utility District

SageGlass

Sasaki

Science Museum of Minnesota

Science Museum of Virginia

Skanska

Sundance Square

Studio One Eleven

SWA

TBG Partners

Tishman Speyer

Toronto Department of Urban Planning

United States Green Building Council

University of Arizona

University of Buffalo

University of California, Berkeley

View Dynamic Glass

Waggonner & Ball

Wheat Design

NOTES

EXECUTIVE SUMMARY

1. Centers for Disease Control and Prevention, National Center for Environmental Health, *Climate Change and Extreme Heat Events,* https://www.cdc.gov/climateandhealth/pubs/ClimateChangeandExtremeHeatEvents.pdf.

PART I: THE SCIENCE AND IMPACTS

1. Earth Science Communication Team, "2018 Fourth Warmest Year in Continued Warming Trend, according to NASA, NOAA," *NASA's Jet Propulsion Laboratory,* July 9, 2019.

2. Sean Breslin, "The Record-Breaking Heat Isn't Just Uncomfortable—It's Killing People," *The Weather Channel,* July 6 2018, https://weather.com/safety/heat/news/2018-07-05-deadly-heat-wave-impacts-us-canada-europe-asia; Alissa Walker, "Our Cities Are Getting Hotter—and It's Killing People," *Curbed,* August 3, 2018, https://www.curbed.com/2018/7/6/17539904/heat-wave-extreme-heat-cities-deadly.

3. Brandon Miller, "Record-Breaking Summer Marches on to the Beat of Climate Change," *CNN,* July 24, 2018, https://www.cnn.com/2018/07/23/world/global-heatwaves-climate-change-wxc/index.html.

4. Cally Carswell, "In This Rapaciously Dry Year, a Quiet Question Grows Louder: What Are We Doing Here?," *High Country News,* August 6, 2018, https://www.hcn.org/issues/50.13/climate-change-drought-dread-and-family-in-the-american-southwest.

5. Brian Stone, The City and the Coming Climate: *Climate Change in the Places We Live* (New York: Cambridge University Press, 2012), 2.

6. M.M. Vogel et al. "Concurrent 2018 Hot Extremes across Northern Hemisphere due to Human-Induced Climate Change," *Earth's Future,* forthcoming, doi: 10.1029/2019EF001189.

7. Brian Stone, *The City and the Coming Climate,* 82.

8. John Walsh and Donald Wuebbles et al., "Chapter 2: Our Changing Climate," in *Climate Change Impacts in the United States: The Third National Climate Assessment,* edited by J. M. Melillo, Teresa Richmond, and G. W. Yohe, U.S. Global Change Research Program, 19–67 (2014), doi:10.7930/J0KW5CXT.

9. Brian Stone, Jeremy J. Jess, and Howard Frumkin, "Urban Form and Extreme Heat Events: Are Sprawling Cities More Vulnerable to Climate Change Than Compact Cities?," *Environmental Health Perspectives* (October 1, 2010), https://ehp.niehs.nih.gov/doi/10.1289/ehp.0901879.

10. David Hondula, telephone interview by Elizabeth Foster, January 17, 2019;

11. Zoe Hamstead, telephone interview by Elizabeth Foster, February 4, 2019.

12. U.S. Environmental Protection Agency, "Urban Heat Island Basics," in *Reducing Urban Heat Islands: Compendium of Strategies* (2008), https://www.epa.gov/sites/production/files/2017-05/documents/reducing_urban_heat_islands_ch_1.pdf.

13. Brian Stone, *The City and the Coming Climate,* 77.

14. U.S. Forest Service, Tree Cover Declining in US, https://www.fs.fed.us/inside-fs/tree-cover-declining-us.

15. Nick Earl, Ian Simmonds, and Nigel Tapper, "Weekly Cycles in Peak Time Temperatures and Urban Heat Island Intensity," *Environmental Research Letters* 11, no. 7 (July 1, 2016), https://iopscience.iop.org/article/10.1088/1748-9326/11/7/074003/meta.

16. Guang J. Zhang, Ming Cai, and Aixue Hu, "Energy consumption and the Unexplained Winter Warming over Northern Asia and North America," *Nature Climate Change* 3 (January 27, 2013): 466¬70, https://www.nature.com/articles/nclimate1803.

17. U.S. Environmental Protection Agency, "Urban Heat Island Basics."

18. Kurt Shickman and Snigdha Garg, "The Current State of Urban Heat Island Mitigation Policy," *ACEEE Summer Study on Energy Efficiency in Buildings* (2016): 11-1 to 11-10, https://aceee.org/files/proceedings/2016/data/papers/11_21.pdf.

19. J.M. Sobstyl et al., "Role of City Texture in Urban Heat Islands at Nighttime," *Physics Review Letters* 120 (March 9, 2018), https://journals.aps.org/prl/abstract/10.1103/PhysRevLett.120.108701; Ping Zhang, Marc Imhoff, Robert Wolfe, and Lahouari Bounoua, "Potential Drivers of Urban Heat Islands in the Northeast USA (PowerPoint, NASA), https://www.nasa.gov/pdf/505254main_zhang.pdf.

20. Adam J. Kalkstein et al., "Heat/Mortality Sensitivities in Los Angeles during Winter: A Unique Phenomenon in the United States," *Environmental Health* 17 (May 3, 2018): 45, https://www.ncbi.nlm.nih.gov/pmc/articles/PMC5934864/.

21. Aric Jenkins, "Here's Why Planes Can't Take Off When It's Too Hot," *Fortune,* June 20, 2017, http://fortune.com/2017/06/20/phoenix-american-airlines-flights-cancelled-heat-wave/.

22. Amy Held, "Melting Roads and Runny Roofs: Heat Scorches the Northern Hemisphere," *NPR,* July 5, 2018, https://www.npr.org/2018/07/05/626057055/melting-roads-and-runny-roofs-heat-scorches-the-northern-hemisphere.

23. Amy Fleming et al. "Heat: The Next Big Inequality Issue," *The Guardian,* August 13, 2018, https://www.preventionweb.net/news/view/59965.

24. Jeremy Hoffman, telephone interview by Elizabeth Foster, April 12, 2019; Maritza Pechin, telephone interview by Elizabeth Foster, April 18, 2019.

25. Virginia Hewitt, Eric Macres, and Kurt Schickman, "Cool Policies for Cool Cities: Best Practices for Mitigating Urban Heat Islands in North American Cities," *ACEEE Summer Study on Energy Efficiency in Buildings* (2014): 10-131 to 10-145, https://aceee.org/files/proceedings/2014/data/papers/10-356.pdf.

26. U.S. Environmental Protection Agency and Centers for Disease Control and Prevention, *Climate Change and Extreme Heat: What You Can Do to Prepare* (October 2016), https://www.cdc.gov/climateandhealth/pubs/extreme-heat-guidebook.pdf.

27. Centers for Disease Control and Prevention, "Heat-Related Illness," https://www.cdc.gov/pictureofamerica/pdfs/picture_of_america_heat-related_illness.pdf.

28. Sara P. Hoverter, *Adapting to Urban Heat: A Tool Kit for Local Governments* (Washington, DC: Georgetown Climate Center, 2012), https://kresge.org/sites/default/files/climate-adaptation-urban-heat.pdf.

29. Global Cool Cities Alliance, Saving Lives, 2017, https://globalcoolcities.org/discover/unlock/unlock-saving-lives/.

30. Riccardo Colacito, Bridget Hoffmann, Toan Phan, and Tim Sablik, "The Impact of Higher Temperatures on Economic Growth" (Federal Reserve Bank of Richmond, August 2018), https://www.richmondfed.org/-/media/richmondfedorg/publications/research/economic_brief/2018/pdf/eb_18-08.pdf.

31. Moody's Investors Service, "Climate Change Is Forecast to Heighten US Exposure to Economic Loss Placing Short-Term and Long-Term Credit Pressure on US States and Local Governments," November 28, 2017, https://www.moodys.com/research/Moodys-Climate-change-is-forecast-to-heighten-US-exposure-to--PR_376056.

32. Moody's Investors Service, "Climate Change Is Forecast to Heighten US Exposure to Economic Loss Placing Short-Term and Long-Term Credit Pressure on US States and Local Governments.

33. Emily Chasan, "Fitch to Start Saying How Climate, Social Issues Affect Ratings," *Bloomberg,* January 7, 2019, https://news.bloombergenvironment.com/environment-and-energy/fitch-to-start-saying-how-climate-social-issues-affect-ratings; S&P Global Ratings, Our Approach to Assessing ESG in Ratings, 2019, https://www.spratings.com/en_US/products/-/product-detail/our-approach-to-esg-in-ratings; S&P Global, "S&P Global Releases Inaugural Climate Disclosure Report Following TCFD Recommendations," *Cision PR Newswire,* May 8, 2019, https://www.prnewswire.com/news-releases/sp-global-releases-inaugural-climate-disclosure-report-following-tcfd-recommendations-300846267.html.

34. Umair Irfan, "Heat Waves Can Be Deadly for Workers and Will Drain the US Economy," *Vox,* July 29, 2018, https://www.vox.com/2018/7/27/17611940/heat-wave-2018-cost-workers-deaths-health-climate-change.

35. Union of Concerned Scientists, Heat Waves and Climate Change: The Effects of Worsening Heat on People, Communities, and Infrastructure, August 2018, https://www.ucsusa.org/sites/default/files/attach/2018/08/extreme-heat-impacts-fact-sheet.pdf.

36. International Council of Shopping Centers, "SoCal Wildfires Challenge Retailers and Landlords," January 5, 2018, https://www.icsc.org/news-and-views/icsc-exchange/socal-wildfires-challenge-retailers-and-landlords.

37. Brian Stone, *The City and the Coming Climate,* 73.

38. U.S.-Canada Power System Outage Task Force, *Final Report on the August 14, 2003 Blackout in the United States and Canada: Causes and Recommendations* (U.S. Department of Energy and Ministry of Natural Resources Canada, April 2004), https://www3.epa.gov/region1/npdes/merrimackstation/pdfs/ar/AR-1165.pdf.

39. Kevin Krajick and Kyu Lee, "Climate Change Has Doubled Western U.S. Forest Fires, Says Study" (Columbia University, The Earth Institute, October 10, 2016), https://www.earth.columbia.edu/articles/view/3343.

40. U.S. Environmental Protection Agency, "Heat Island Impacts," March 1, 2019, https://www.epa.gov/heat-islands/heat-island-impacts#water.

PART II: IMPLICATIONS AND OPPORTUNITIES FOR THE REAL ESTATE SECTOR

1. Global Cool Cities Alliance, Energy Savings 2017, https://globalcoolcities.org/discover/unlock/unlock-energy-savings/.

2. R. Levinson, H. Akbari, S. Konopacki, and S. Bretz, "Inclusion of Cool Roofs in Nonresidential Title 24 Prescriptive Requirements" (Paper LBNL-50451, Lawrence Berkeley National Laboratory, Berkeley, CA, 2002).

3. A. Tzavali, John Paravantis, Giouli MIhalakakou, Aleksandr Epaminond Fotiadi, and Eleni Stigka, "Urban Heat Island Intensity: A Literature Review," *Fresenius Environmental Bulletin* (2015), https://www.researchgate.net/publication/298083233_Urban_heat_island_intensity_A_literature_review/download.

4. Heat Island Group of Lawrence Berkeley National Lab, "Cool Pavements," 2019, https://heatisland.lbl.gov/coolscience/cool-pavements.

5. U.S. Environmental Protection Agency, "Using Cool Roofs to Reduce Heat Islands," August 12, 2016, https://www.epa.gov/heat-islands/using-cool-roofs-reduce-heat-islands.

6. U.S. Environmental Protection Agency, "Using Green Roofs to Reduce Heat Islands," March 1, 2019, https://www.epa.gov/heat-islands/using-green-roofs-reduce-heat-islands.

7. GSA, "Green Roofs," https://www.gsa.gov/about-us/organization/office-of-governmentwide-policy/office-of-federal-highperformance-buildings/resource-library/integrative-strategies/green-roofs; GSA, "Cost Benefit Analysis," in *The Benefits and Challenges of Green Roofs on Public and Commercial Buildings* (2011), 67–76, https://www.gsa.gov/cdnstatic/Cost_Benefit_Analysis.pdf.

8. Richard Conniff, "U.S. Cities Lose Tree Cover Just When They Need It Most," *Scientific American,* May 7, 2018, https://www.scientificamerican.com/article/u-s-cities-lose-tree-cover-just-when-they-need-it-most/?redirect=1.

9. UK Green Building Council, *Health, Wellbeing & Productivity in Offices* (London: World Green Building Council, 2014).

10. Jay, "Why Seattle Rental Property Owners Are Considering A/C?," *Real Property Associates* blog, May 27, 2017, https://rpapropertymanagementblog.com/why-seattle-rental-property-owners-considering-ac/.

11. "BOMA 2016 Experience Exchange Reports Released," *Facility Executive,* July 22, 2016, https://facilityexecutive.com/2016/07/boma-2016-experience-exchange-reports/; A. Tzavali, John Paravantis, Giouli MIhalakakou, Aleksandr Epaminond Fotiadi, and Eleni Stigka, "Urban Heat Island Intensity: A Literature Review," *Fresenius Environmental Bulletin* (2015), https://www.researchgate.net/publication/298083233_Urban_heat_island_intensity_A_literature_review/download.

12. U.S. Global Change Research Program, "Increase in Cooling Demand and Decrease in Heating Demand," in *National Climate Assessment,* April 28, 2014, https://nca2014.globalchange.gov/highlights/report-findings/infrastructure/graphics/increase-cooling-demand-and-decrease-heating.

13. BlackRock Investment Institute, "Getting Physical: Assessing Climate Risks," April 4, 2019, https://www.blackrock.com/us/individual/insights/blackrock-investment-institute/physical-climate-risks.

14. Better Bricks, "Case Study: Smart Windows Are Smart Business," Northwest Energy Efficiency Alliance, https://betterbricks.com/uploads/resources/Lake-Union-Building-Case-Study_0.pdf.

15. Benjamin Collier, "Small and Young Businesses Are Especially Vulnerable to Extreme Weather," *Harvard Business Review,* November 23, 2016, https://hbr.org/2016/11/small-and-young-businesses-are-especially-vulnerable-to-extreme-weather.

16. Rebecca J. Rosen, "Keepin' It Cool: How the Air Conditioner Made Modern America," *The Atlantic,* July 14, 2011, https://www.theatlantic.com/technology/archive/2011/07/keepin-it-cool-how-the-air-conditioner-made-modern-america/241892/.

17. Francisco Estrada, W.J. Wouter Botzen, and Richard S.J. Tol, "A Global Economic Assessment of City Policies to Reduce Climate Change Impacts," *Nature,* May 29, 2017, https://www.nature.com/articles/nclimate3301.

18. K. Hayhoe et al. (2010), cited in *Climate Change and Infrastructure, Urban Systems, and Vulnerabilities: Technical Report for the U.S. Department of Energy in Support of the National Climate Assessment,* edited by Thomas J. Wilbanks and Steven J. Fernandez (Washington, DC: Island Press, 2013), 7, https://www.eenews.net/assets/2014/03/06/document_cw_01.pdf.

19. Amy Held, "Melting Roads and Runny Roofs: Heat Scorches the Northern Hemisphere," *NPR,* July 5, 2018, https://www.npr.org/2018/07/05/626057055/melting-roads-and-runny-roofs-heat-scorches-the-northern-hemisphere.

20. Michael Granberry, "Museum Tower Glare Put the Nasher in the Hot Seat Seven Years Ago. Arts Patrons Still Wonder When We'll See a Fix," *Dallas Morning News,* October 25, 2018, https://www.dallasnews.com/arts/museums/2018/10/25/seven-years-after-museum-tower-glare-put-nasher-hot-seat-arts-patrons-still-wondering-isnt-something-done.

21. Brad Plumer, "Companies See Climate Change Hitting Their Bottom Lines in the Next 5 Years," *New York Times,* June 4, 2019, https://www.nytimes.com/2019/06/04/climate/companies-climate-change-financial-impact.html.

22. Megan Garber, "Wait, Tarmac Can *Melt*?," *The Atlantic,* July 9, 2012, https://www.theatlantic.com/technology/archive/2012/07/wait-tarmac-can-melt/259565/.

23. Zach Wichter, "Too Hot to Fly?," *New York Times,* June 20, 2017, https://www.nytimes.com/2017/06/20/business/flying-climate-change.html.

24. City of Cincinnati, *2018 Green Cincinnati Plan,* adopted May 2018, 188, https://www.cincinnati-oh.gov/oes/assets/File/2018%20Green%20Cincinnati%20Plan(1).pdf.

25. Kendra Pierre-Louis, "The World Wants Air-Conditioning. That Could Warm the World," *New York Times,* May 15, 2018, https://www.nytimes.com/2018/05/15/climate/air-conditioning.html.

26. U.S. Energy Information Administration, "Air Conditioning Accounts for About 12% of U.S. Home Energy Expenditures," *Today in Energy,* July 23, 2018, https://www.eia.gov/todayinenergy/detail.php?id=36692.

27. Brian Stone, *The City and the Coming Climate: Climate Change in the Places We Live* (New York: Cambridge University Press, 2012), 13.

28. Farshid Aram, Ester Higueras Garcia, Ebrahim Solgi, and Soran Mansournia, "Urban Green Space Cooling Effect in Cities," *Heliyon* 5 (April 8, 2019), https://www.ncbi.nlm.nih.gov/pmc/articles/PMC6458494/; Food and Agriculture Organization of the United Nations, "Rethinking the Future of Cities: How Trees Are Revolutionizing Cities around the World," 2019, www.fao.org/fao-stories/article/en/c/1106849/.

29. Global Cool Cities Alliance, Unlock the Benefits of Reflective Cool Roofs, Saving Lives, 2017, https://globalcoolcities.org/discover/unlock/unlock-saving-lives/.

30. Jiachuan Yang, Zhihua Wang, and Kamil E. Kaloush, "Unintended Consequences: A Research Synthesis Examining the Use of Reflective Pavements to Mitigate the Urban Heat Island Effect" (White Paper, Arizona State University National Center of Excellence for SMART Innovations, October 2013).

31. Phoenix Rising Football Club, "Phoenix Rising Football Club Selects Populous, Gould Evans Architectural firms to Design Proposed Major League Soccer Stadium," *Cision PR Newswire,* January 23, 2018, https://www.prnewswire.com/news-releases/phoenix-rising-football-club-selects-populous-gould-evans-architectural-firms-to-design-proposed-major-league-soccer-stadium-300586953.html.

32. Marissa Payne, "The Artificial Turf at the Women's World Cup Was Reportedly 120 Degrees at Kick Off," *Washington Post,* June 6, 2015, https://www.washingtonpost.com/news/early-lead/wp/2015/06/06/the-artificial-turf-at-the-womens-world-cup-was-reportedly-120-degrees-at-kick-off/?utm_term=.dff09d4d822d.

33. Bautex, "Designing Energy Efficient Buildings in Hot Climates," https://www.bautexsystems.com/blog/hot-climate-building-design.

34. New Zealand Ministry of Business, Innovation & Employment (Hikina Whakatotuki), Smart Guide: Using Thermal Mass for Heating and Cooling, https://www.smarterhomes.org.nz/smart-guides/design/thermal-mass-for-heating-and-cooling/; Zero Energy Project, Construction & Design Considerations in Warmer Climates, https://zeroenergyproject.org/warmer-climate-construction-design-considerations/.

35. ECHOtape, "Contractors Field Guide to the Building Envelope," October 9, 2018, https://www.echotape.com/blog/contractors-field-guide-building-envelope/.

36. Doris Osterreicher and Stefan Sattler, "Maintaining Comfortable Summertime Indoor Temperatures by Means of Passive Design Measures to Mitigate the Urban Heat Island Effect—A Sensitivity Analysis for Residential Buildings in the City of Vienna," *Urban Science* 2, no. 3 (August 8, 2019): 66, https://www.mdpi.com/2413-8851/2/3/66/htm.

37. U.S. Environmental Protection Agency, "Cool Roofs," in *Reducing Urban Heat Islands: Compendium of Strategies* (2008), https://www.epa.gov/sites/production/files/2017-05/documents/reducing_urban_heat_islands_ch_4.pdf.

38. The Heat Island Group at Lawrence Berkeley National Lab, Cool Pavements, 2019, https://heatisland.lbl.gov/coolscience/cool-pavements.

39. Neda Yaghoobian and Jan Kleissl, "Effect of Reflective Pavements on Building Energy Use," *Urban Climate* 2 (December 2012): 25–42, https://www.sciencedirect.com/science/article/pii/S2212095512000077.

40. Paul Osmond and Ehsan Sharifi, Guide to Urban Cooling Strategies (Low Carbon Living CRC, Australia, July 2017), http://www.lowcarbonlivingcrc.com.au/sites/all/files/publications_file_attachments/rp2024_guide_to_urban_cooling_strategies_2017_web.pdf.

41. U.S. Government Accountability Office, "School Facilities: America's School's Not Designed or Equipped for 21st Century," April 4, 1995, https://www.gao.gov/products/HEHS-95-95.

42. J.M. Sobstyl, T. Emig, Qomi M.J. Abdolhosseini, F.-J. Ulm, and R.J.-M. Pellenq, "Role of City Texture in Urban Heat Islands at Nighttime," *Physics Review Letters,* March 9, 2018, https://journals.aps.org/prl/abstract/10.1103/PhysRevLett.120.108701.

43. Ping Zhang, Marc Imhoff, Robert Wolfe, and Lahouari Bounoua, "Potential Drivers of Urban Heat Islands in the Northeast USA," National Aeronautics and Space Administration (NASA), https://www.nasa.gov/pdf/505254main_zhang.pdf.

44. U.S. Environmental Protection Agency, "Urban Heat Island Basics," in *Reducing Urban Heat Islands: Compendium of Strategies* (2008), https://www.epa.gov/sites/production/files/2014-06/documents/basicscompendium.pdf.

45. Richard Conniff, "U.S. Cities Lose Tree Cover Just When They Need It Most," *Scientific American,* May 7, 2018, https://www.scientificamerican.com/article/u-s-cities-lose-tree-cover-just-when-they-need-it-most/.

46. Tim Newcomb, "Portland's Sellwood Bridge Earns Highest Greenroads Score to Date," *ENR Northwest* blog, December 1, 2017, https://www.enr.com/blogs/15-evergreen/post/43539-portlands-sellwood-bridge-earns-highest-greenroads-score-to-date.

47. Greenroads, Bagby Street Reconstruction, https://www.greenroads.org/141/49/bagby-street-reconstruction.html; Design Workshop, Bagby Street Reconstruction, 2018, www.designworkshop.com/projects/bagby.html.

48. U.S. Department of Housing and Urban Development, FY2015–2016 Planning Grant Award Information. Choice Neighborhoods, Phoenix, Arizona, https://www.phoenix.gov/housingsite/Documents/CNI_planninggrantees2015.pdf.

49. LISC Phoenix and Vitalyst Health Foundation, Executive Summary, *Edison Eastlake Community Choice Neighborhood Initiative Health Impact Assessment* (Phoenix, 2017), www.liscphoenix.org/wp-content/uploads/2017/11/EEC_HIA_FINAL.pdf; Heat Action Planning Guide for Neighborhoods of Greater Phoenix Draft (Maricopa County Public Health, The Nature Conservancy, et al.).

50. "Phoenix Gets $30M Grant to Remake Edison-Eastlake Neightborhood East of Downtown," *AZcentral,* July 20, 2018, https://www.azcentral.com/story/news/local/phoenix/2018/07/20/edison-eastlake-neighborhood-phoenix-gets-30-million-hud-grant/804547002/.

51. LISC Phoenix and Vitalyst Health Foundation, Executive Summary, *Edison Eastlake Community Choice Neighborhood Initiative Health Impact Assessment,* www.liscphoenix.org/wp-content/uploads/2017/11/EEC-HIA-ExecSummary.pdf.

52. LISC Phoenix and Vitalyst Health Foundation, Executive Summary, *Edison Eastlake Community Choice Neighborhood Initiative Health Impact Assessment,* www.liscphoenix.org/wp-content/uploads/2017/11/EEC-HIA-ExecSummary.pdf.

53. "Gorman Partners with Phoenix on $30 Million HUD Grant," NH&RA, *HousingOnline Weekly,* July 25, 2018, https://www.housingonline.com/2018/07/25/gorman-partners-with-phoenix-on-30-million-hud-grant/.

54. Office of Environmental Quality, Transportation and Environmental Services, City of Alexandria Energy and Climate Change Action Plan (draft), March 14, 2011, https://www.alexandriava.gov/uploadedFiles/tes/eco-city/DraftEnergyClimateActionPlan03.14.2011.pdf.

55. District of Columbia, *Climate Ready DC,* November 15, 2016, https://doee.dc.gov/sites/default/files/dc/sites/ddoe/service_content/attachments/CRDC-Report-FINAL-Web.pdf.

56. JBG Smith, *Amazon HQ at National Landing Update,* December 2018, http://investors.jbgsmith.com/Cache/1001246278.PDF?O=PDF&T=&Y=&D=&FID=1001246278&iid=4899055.

57. Alex Koma, "JBG Smith Launches New Experiment to Cool Down Crystal City Parking Lots," *ARLnow,* October 16, 2018, https://www.arlnow.com/2018/10/16/jbg-smith-launches-new-experiment-to-cool-down-crystal-city-parking-lots/.

58. Koma, "JBG Smith Launches New Experiment to Cool Down Crystal City Parking Lots."

59. ASU SkySong Innovation Center website, https://fabritecstructures.com/portfolio/asu-skysong-innovation-center/.

60. "CICEP 2016 Case Study, Arizona State University," https://www.aplu.org/projects-and-initiatives/economic-development-and-community-engagement/innovation-and-economic-prosperity-universities-designation-and-awards-program/IEP_Library/skysong--the-asu-scottsdale-innovation-center/file.

PART III: THE EXTREME HEAT POLICY LANDSCAPE

1. U.S. Environmental Protection Agency, "Cool Roofs," in *Reducing Urban Heat Islands: Compendium of Strategies* (2008), https://www.epa.gov/sites/production/files/2017-05/documents/reducing_urban_heat_islands_ch_4.pdf; "Portland Adopts a Green Roof Requirement in the Central City 2035 Plan," *Living Architecture Monitor,* June 14, 2018, https://livingarchitecturemonitor.com/news/2018/6/14/portland-adopts-a-green-roof-requirement-in-the-central-city-2035-plan.

2. Virginia Hewitt, Eric Mackres, and Kurt Shickman, "Cool Policies for Cool Cities: Best Practices for Mitigating Urban Heat Islands in North American Cities" (ACEEE Summer Study on Energy Efficiency in Buildings, 2014), https://aceee.org/files/proceedings/2014/data/papers/10-356.pdf.

3. Telephone interviews by Elizabeth Foster with Larry Falkin, sustainability director of Cincinnati's Office of Environment and Sustainability, December 17, 2018, and with Marie Light, program manager for the Pima County Department of Environmental Quality, February 4, 2019.

4. "Moody's - Largest US Cities Take Proactive Steps to Mitigate Credit Risk from Climate Change," Moody's Investors Service, January 17, 2019, https://www.moodys.com/research/Moodys-Largest-US-cities-take-proactive-steps-to-mitigate-credit--PBM_1158519.

5. Greg Kats and Keith Glassbrook, *Delivering Urban Resilience* (Washington, DC: U.S. Green Building Council, 2018), https://www.usgbc.org/sites/default/files/delivering-urban-resilience-2018.pdf.

6. Deborah Netburn, "L.A.'s Mayor Wants to Lower the City's Temperature. These Scientists Are Figuring Out How to Do It," *Los Angeles Times,* February 9, 2017, https://www.latimes.com/projects/la-sci-cooling-los-angeles/; Neil McMahon, "Can Melbourne Lower Its Temperature by 7 Degrees?," *Citylab,* February 2, 2015, https://www.citylab.com/environment/2015/02/can-melbourne-lower-its-temperature-by-7-degrees/385050/.

7. Neil McMahon, "Can Melbourne Lower Its Temperature by 7 Degrees?"

8. Eric Garcetti, "Mayor Garcetti Announces New $100 Million Insulation Rebate Program," Los Angeles Mayor's Office, August 24, 2018, https://www.lamayor.org/mayor-garcetti-announces-new-100-million-insulation-rebate-program.

9. Telephone interview by Elizabeth Foster with David Mercuris, senior vice president of development and communications, Goldenberg Development, February 2, 2019; Philadelphia Water Department, Green Stormwater Infrastructure Tools, 2018, www.phillywatersheds.org/what_were_doing/green_infrastructure/tools.

10. Cool Roof Rating Council, Wall Ratings Expansion Concept (presentation at Annual Membership Meeting, Sacramento, CA, May 18, 2018), https://coolroofs.org/documents/Exhibit_8_-_Cool_Walls_Expansion_Concept.pdf.

11. Sara P. Hoverter, *Adapting to Urban Heat: A Tool Kit for Local Governments* (Washington, DC: Georgetown Climate Center, 2012), https://kresge.org/sites/default/files/climate-adaptation-urban-heat.pdf.

12. City of New York, *Cool Neighborhoods NYC,* https://www1.nyc.gov/assets/orr/pdf/Cool_Neighborhoods_NYC_Report_FINAL.pdf.

13. 100 Resilient Cities and Government of the District of Columbia, *Resilient DC: A Strategy to Thrive in the Face of Change,* May 2019, 82, https://app.box.com/s/d40hk5ltvcn9fqas1viaje0xbnbsfwga.

14. Occupational Heat Exposure, OSHA, https://www.osha.gov/SLTC/heatstress/.

15. Jackson Lewis P.C., "California's Upcoming Indoor Heat Regulation," *OSHA Law Blog,* March 6, 2017, https://www.oshalawblog.com/2017/03/articles/californias-upcoming-indoor-heat-regulation/.

16. Daniel Homsey and Daniel Aldrich, "Neighborfest: Building a Stronger, More Connected World from the Block Up," posted by Amos Stoltzfus, Sept. 12, 2017, at Nextdoor for Public Agencies Resource Center, https://medium.com/nextdooragencyresources/neighborfest-fc6fcd90f6b8; telephone interview by Elizabeth Foster with Daniel Homsey, director of neighborhood resilience, City and County of San Francisco, April 26, 2019.

17. AdaptNY, "Case Study: Deadly Chicago Heat Wave of 1995," 2014, https://www.adaptny.org/2016/07/21/case-study-deadly-chicago-heat-wave-of-1995/.

18. "Dying Alone," an interview with Eric Klinenberg, author of *Heat Wave* (University of Chicago, 2002), https://www.press.uchicago.edu/Misc/Chicago/443213in.html.; Mike Thomas, "An Oral History: Heat Wave," *Chicago,* June 29, 2015, https://www.chicagomag.com/Chicago-Magazine/July-2015/1995-Chicago-heat-wave/.

19. Eric Klinenberg, *Heat Wave: A Social Autopsy of Disaster in Chicago* (Chicago, University of Chicago Press, 2002, 2015), xxiv.

20. 100 Resilient Cities and Government of the District of Columbia, *Resilient DC,* 102.

21. Global Cool Cities Alliance, Urban Heat Island Policy Survey, homepage, https://globalcoolcities.org/urban-heat-island-policy-survey/.

22. Hoverter, *Adapting to Urban Heat;* Sacramento Municipal Utility District, Free Shade Tree Program, https://www.smud.org/en/Going-Green/Free-Shade-Trees.

23. Michelle de la Uz, "CityViews: Act Now to Prevent Heat Deaths and Build a Greener Gowanus," *CityLimits.org,* January 18, 2018, https://citylimits.org/2018/01/18/cityviews-act-now-to-prevent-heat-deaths-and-build-a-greener-gowanus/.

24. Climate Central, "Hot and Getting Hotter: Heat Islands Cooking U.S. Cities," August 20, 2014, https://www.climatecentral.org/news/urban-heat-islands-threaten-us-health-17919.

25. Households reporting air conditioning, NYC Environment & Health Data Portal, http://a816-dohbesp.nyc.gov/IndicatorPublic/VisualizationData.aspx?id=2185,719b87,107,Summarize; Sarah Gonzalez, "Without AC, Public Housing Residents Swelter through the Summer," *WNYC News,* July 28, 2016, https://www.wnyc.org/story/life-new-york-public-housing-no-air-conditioning/.

26. "In Celebration of Earth Day, City Announces Installation of over 10 Million Square Feet of Energy-Saving Rooftops" (press release, NYC Small Business Services, April 22, 2019), https://www1.nyc.gov/site/sbs/about/pr20190422_NYCCoolRoofs.page.

27. C40 Cities, "Case Study: City of Toronto's Eco-Roof Incentive Program and Green Roof Bylaw," December 13 2018, https://www.c40.org/case_studies/city-of-toronto-s-eco-roof-incentive-program-and-green-roof-bylaw.

28. Telephone interview by Elizabeth Foster with Jonathan Parfrey, executive director, Climate Resolve, March 22, 2019.

29. U.S. Green Building Council, definition of SRI, https://www.usgbc.org/glossary/term/5590; superadmin, "What's SRI?," *GAF ProBlog,* March 12, 2013, http://blog.gaf.com/whats-sri/.

30. ResilientCA.org, "Urban Cooling Strategies for Los Angeles Neighborhoods Serviced by the Orange Line," Governor's Office of Planning & Research, State of California, 2019, https://resilientca.org/case-studies/urban-cooling-strategies-for-los-angeles/.

31. ResilientCA.org, "Urban Cooling Strategies for Los Angeles Neighborhoods Serviced by the Orange Line," Governor's Office of Planning & Research, State of California, 2019, https://resilientca.org/case-studies/urban-cooling-strategies-forlos-angeles/.

32. Climate Central, "Hot and Getting Hotter: Heat Islands Cooking U.S. Cities" (research report, August 20, 2014), https://www.climatecentral.org/news/urban-heat-islands-threaten-us-health-17919.

33. Alternative Revenue Work Group, "Alternative Revenue and the City of Madison Proposal for an Urban Forestry Charge," August 2014, https://www.cityofmadison.com/sites/default/files/news/attachments/august_2014_alternative_revenue_urban_forestry_repor.pdf; telephone interview by Elizabeth Foster with Robin Hunt, urban forestry specialist, May 21, 2019.

CONCLUSION: BUILDING FOR A WARMER FUTURE

1. Trevor Nace, "So Far 2019 Has Set 33 Hottest and 0 Coldest Temperature Records," *Forbes,* January 31, 2019, https://www.forbes.com/sites/trevornace/2019/01/31/so-far-2019-has-set-33-hottest-and-0-coldest-temperature-records/#15880269505e.

There is significant opportunity for the public and private real estate and land use sectors to mitigate and adapt to extreme heat to make American cities more resilient and livable today and in the future.